I SEE FACES

I SEE FACES

LANNOO

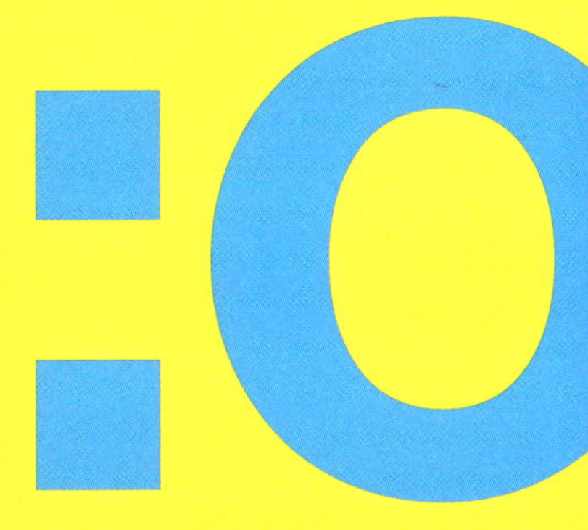

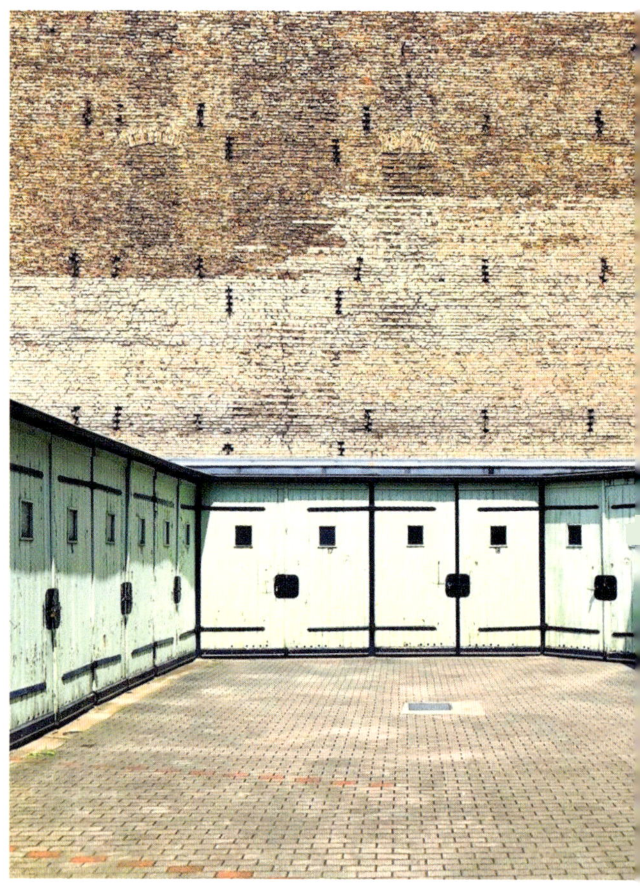

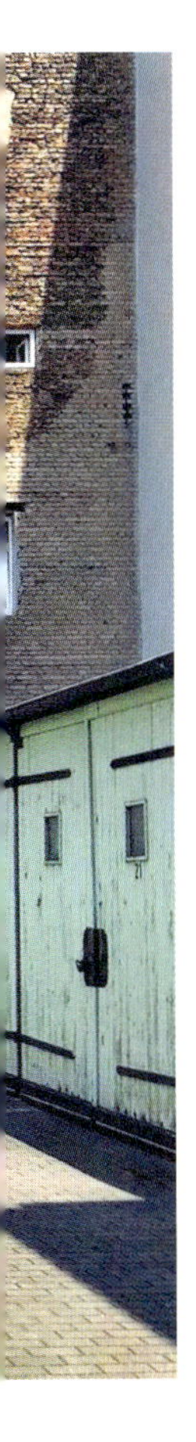

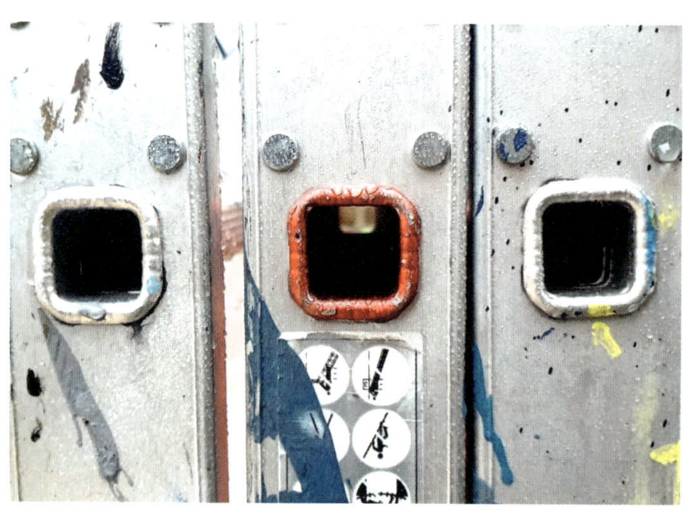

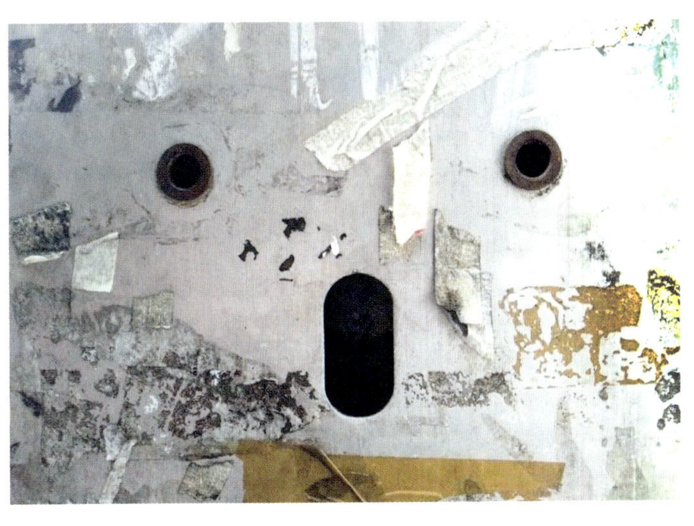

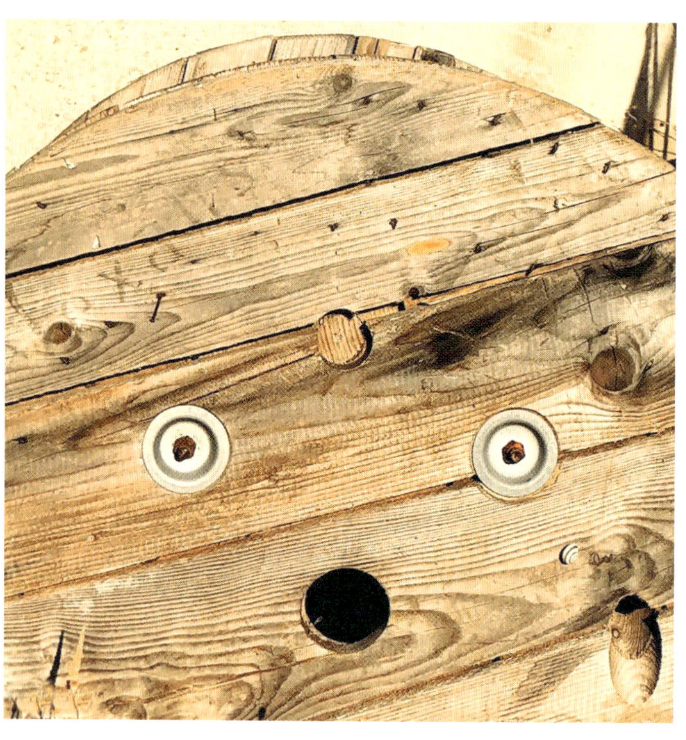

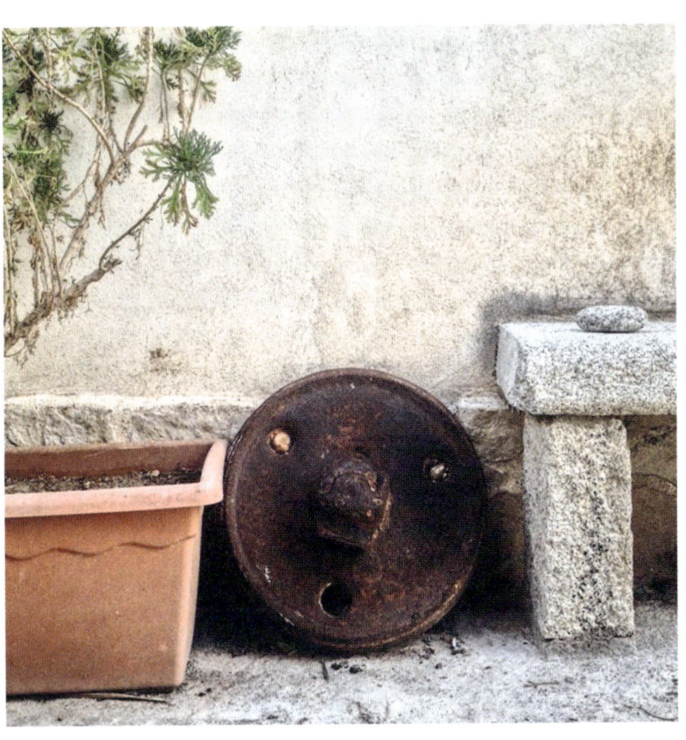

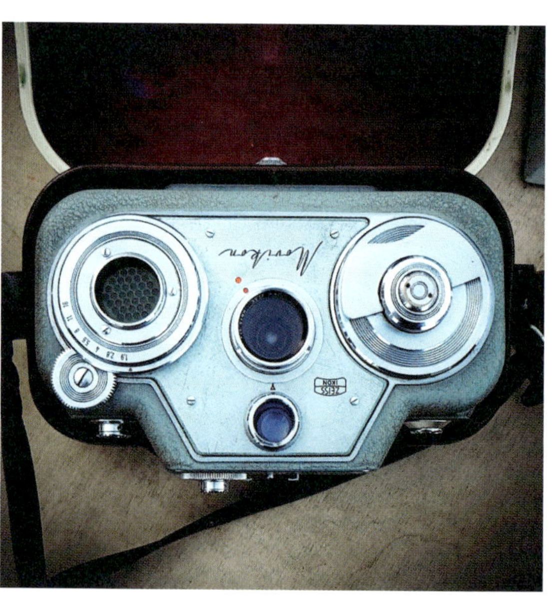
Movikon
ZEISS IKON

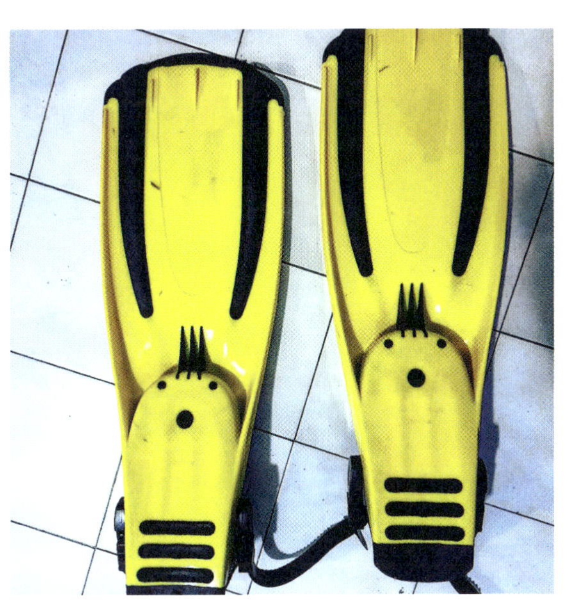

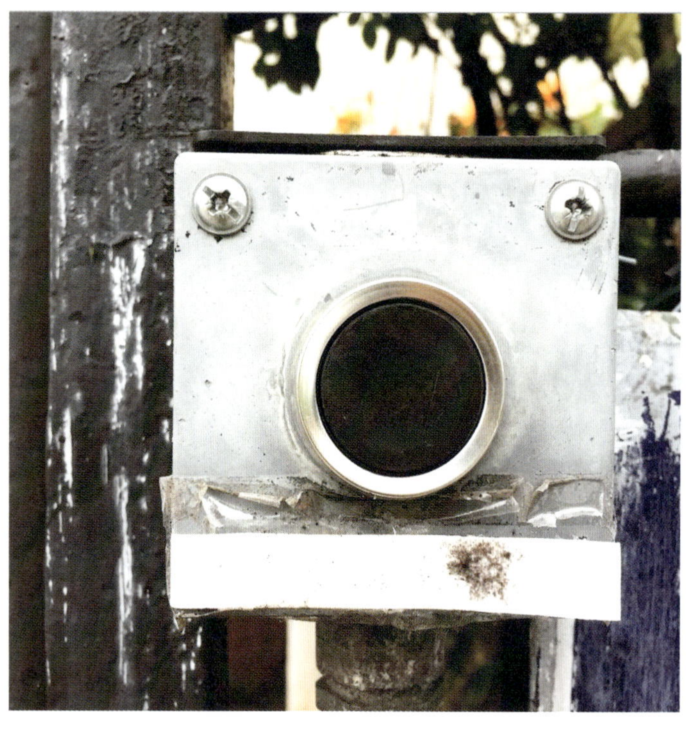

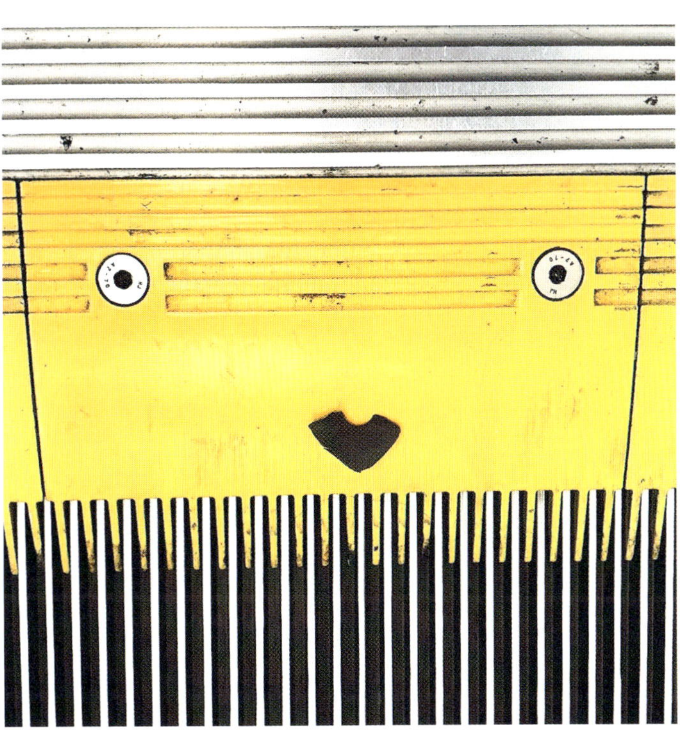

I SEE

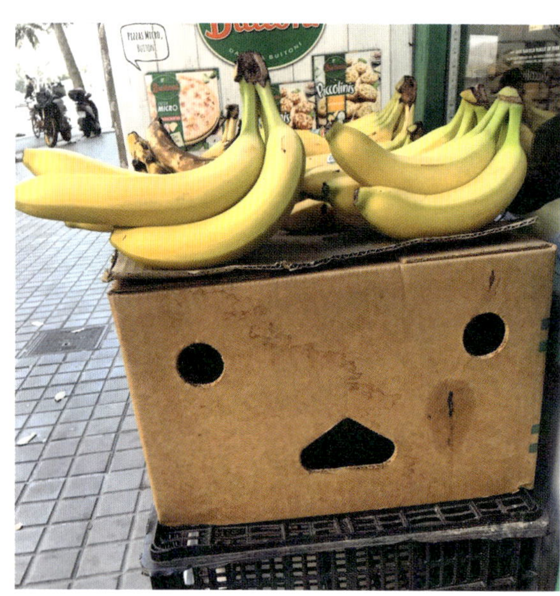

IN

FACES

THINGS

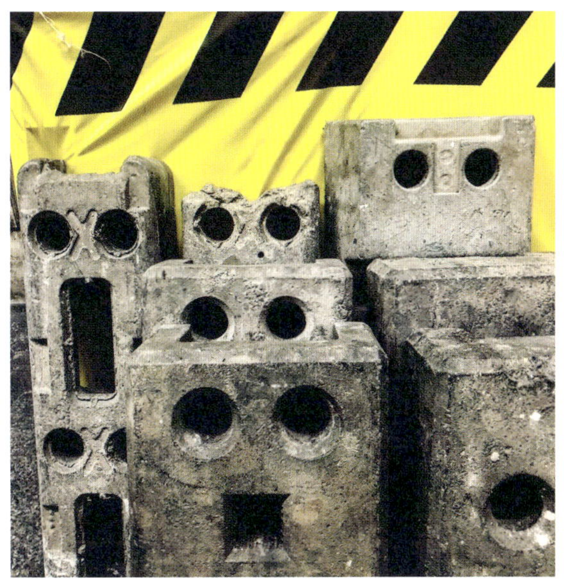

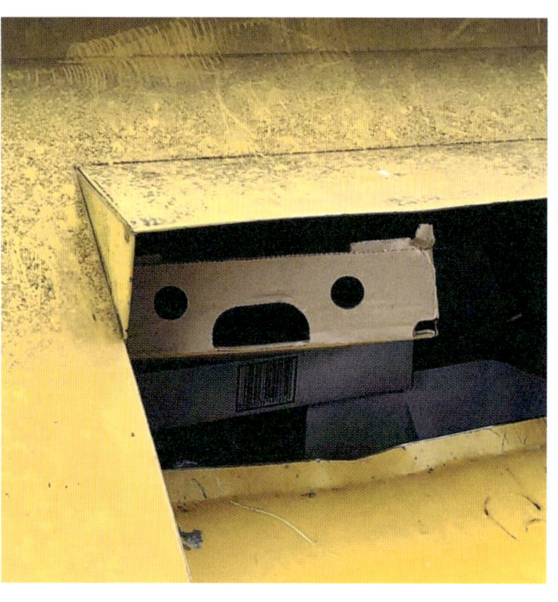

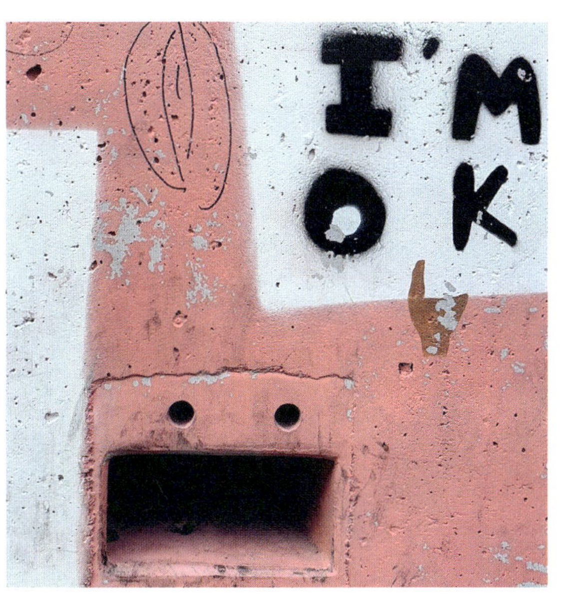
I'M
OK

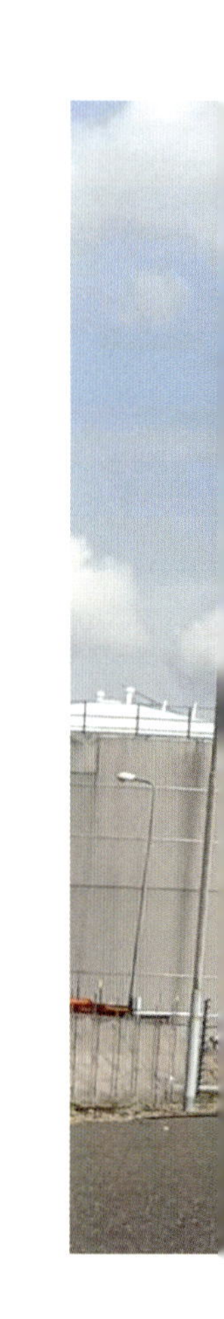

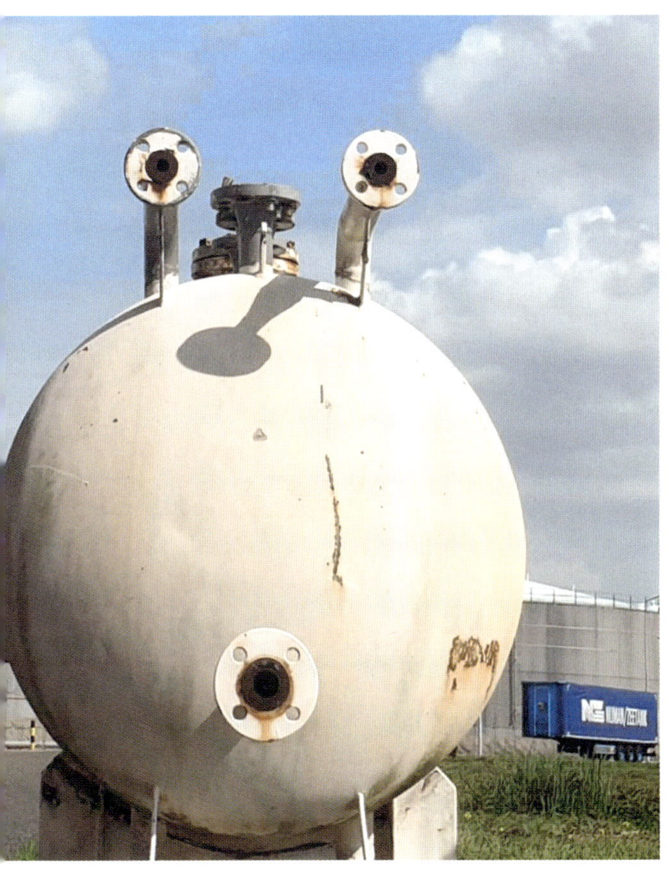

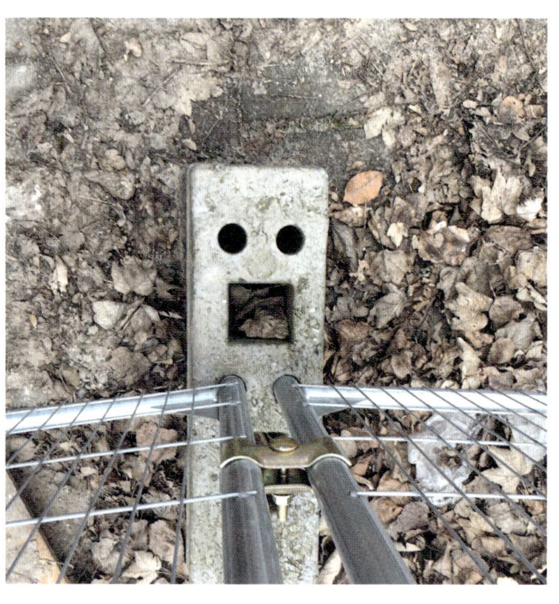

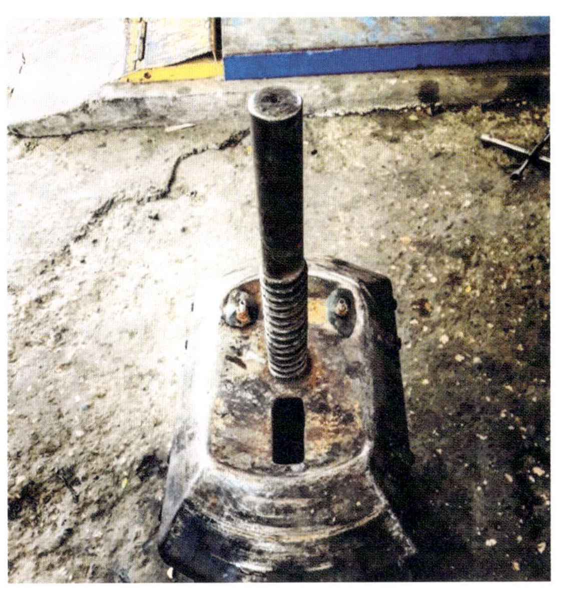

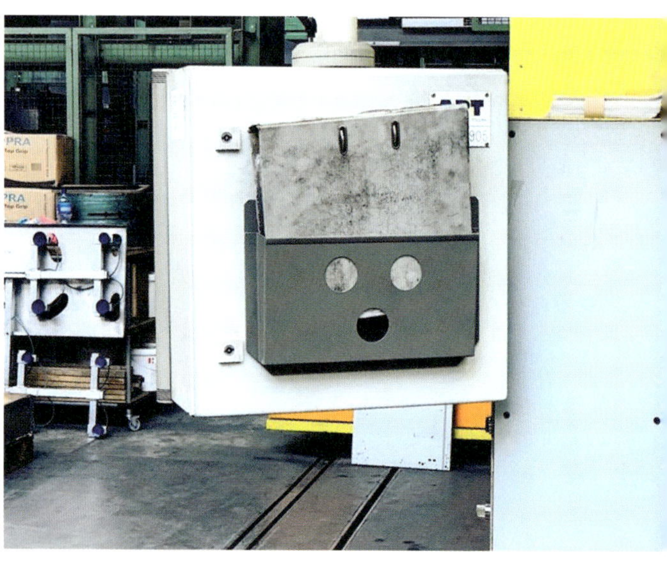

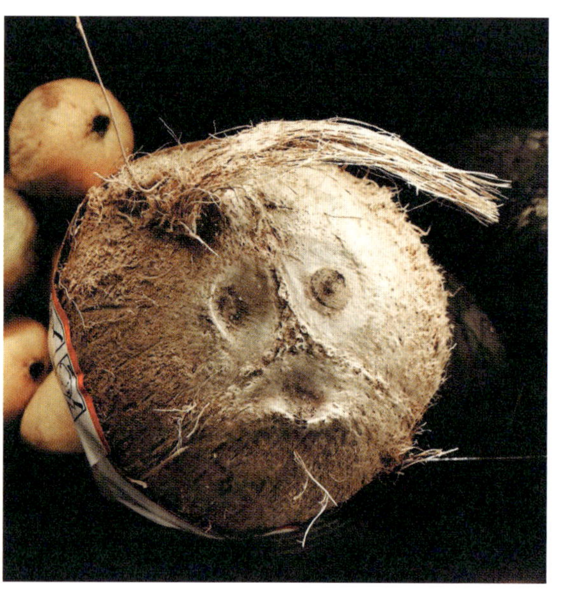

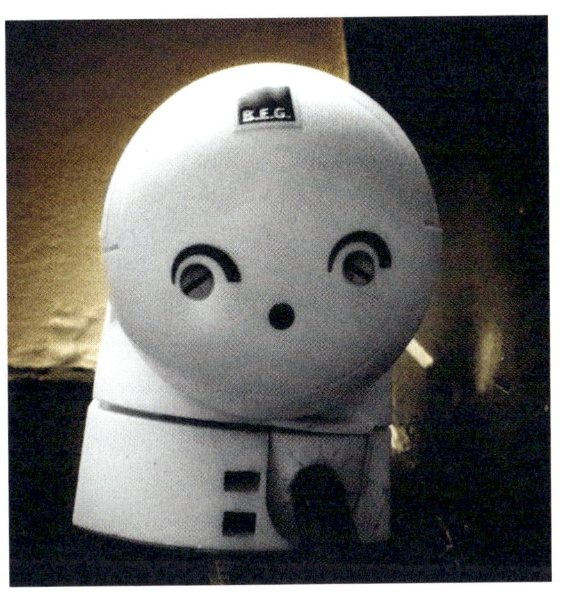
B.E.G.

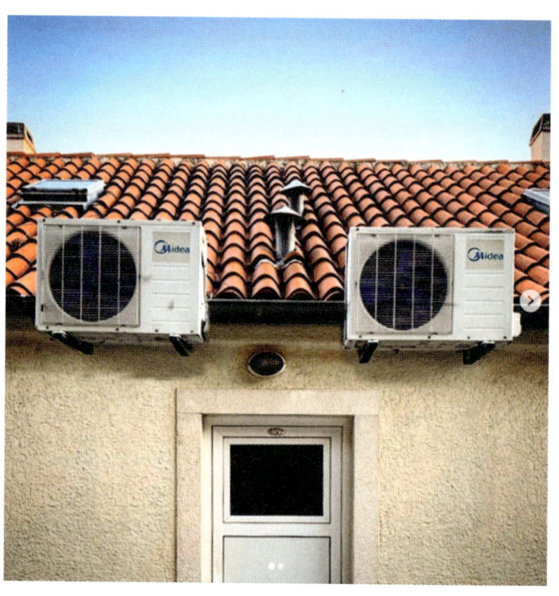
Midea
Midea

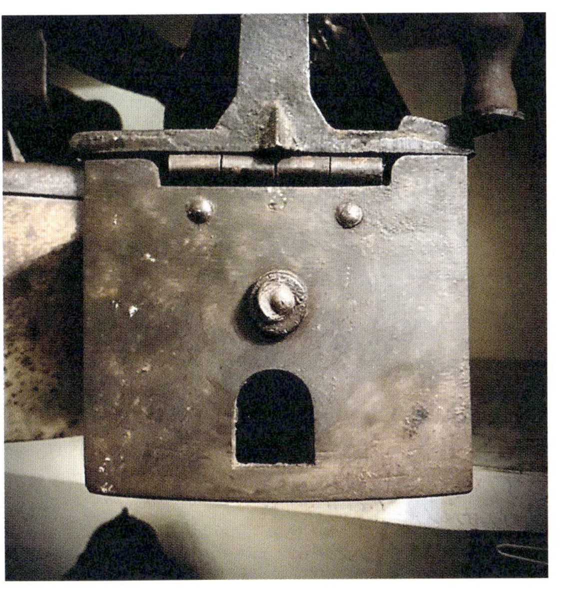

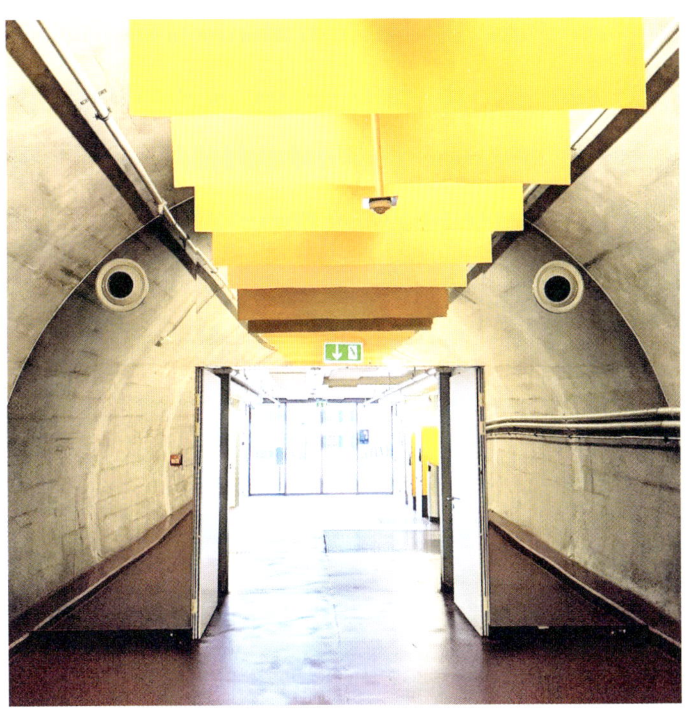

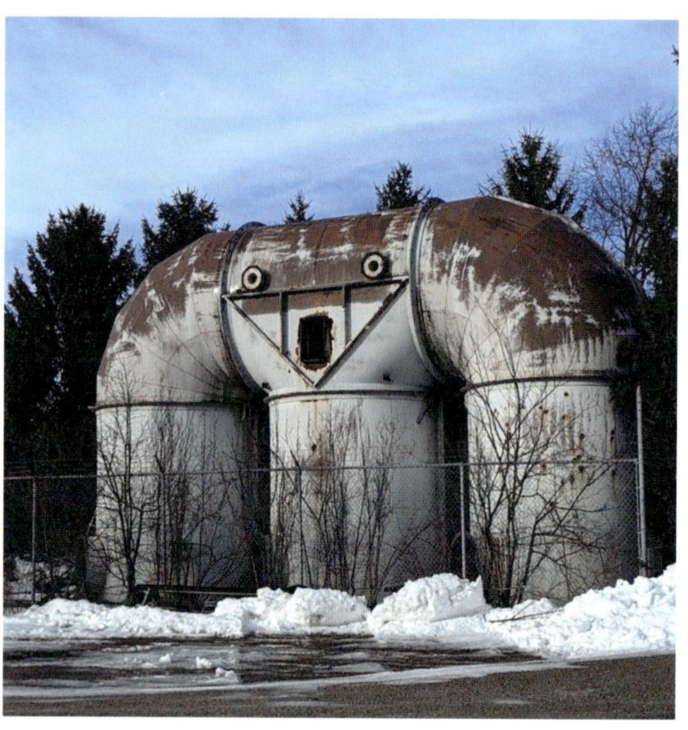

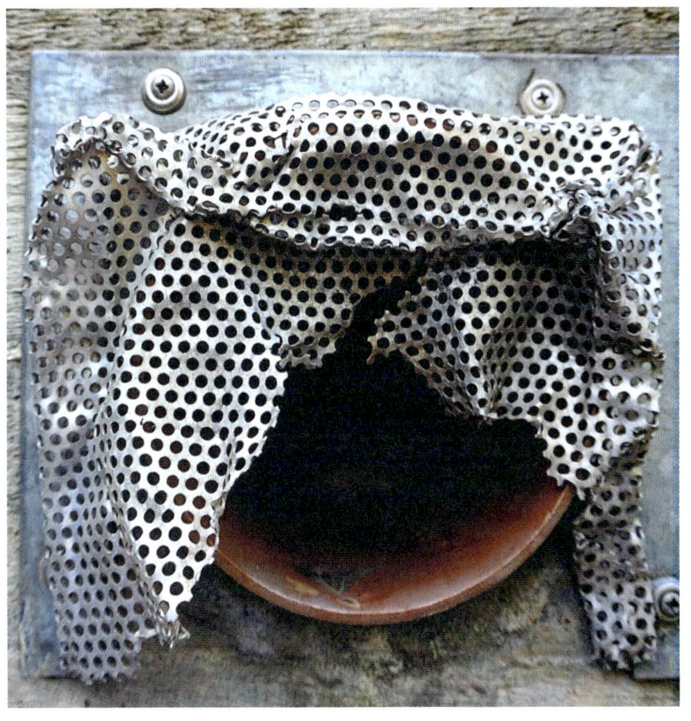

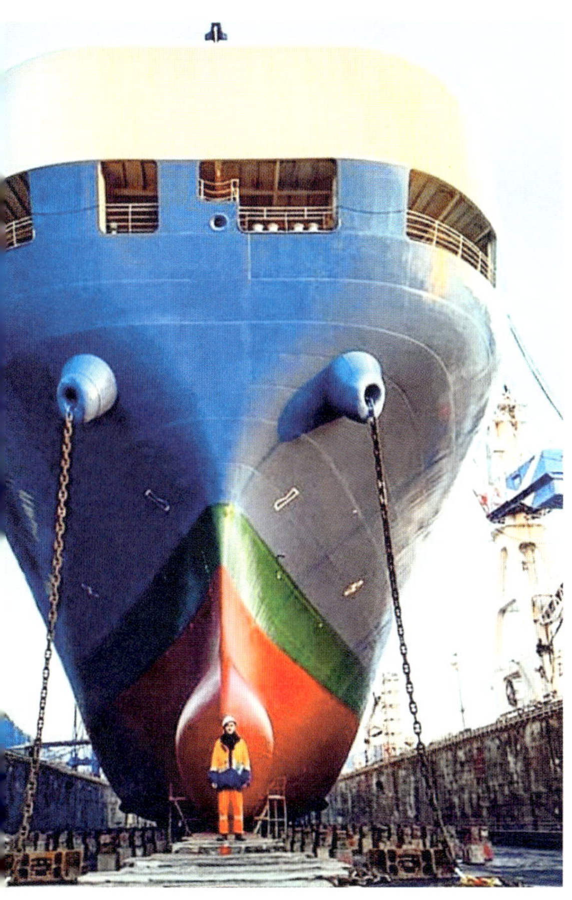

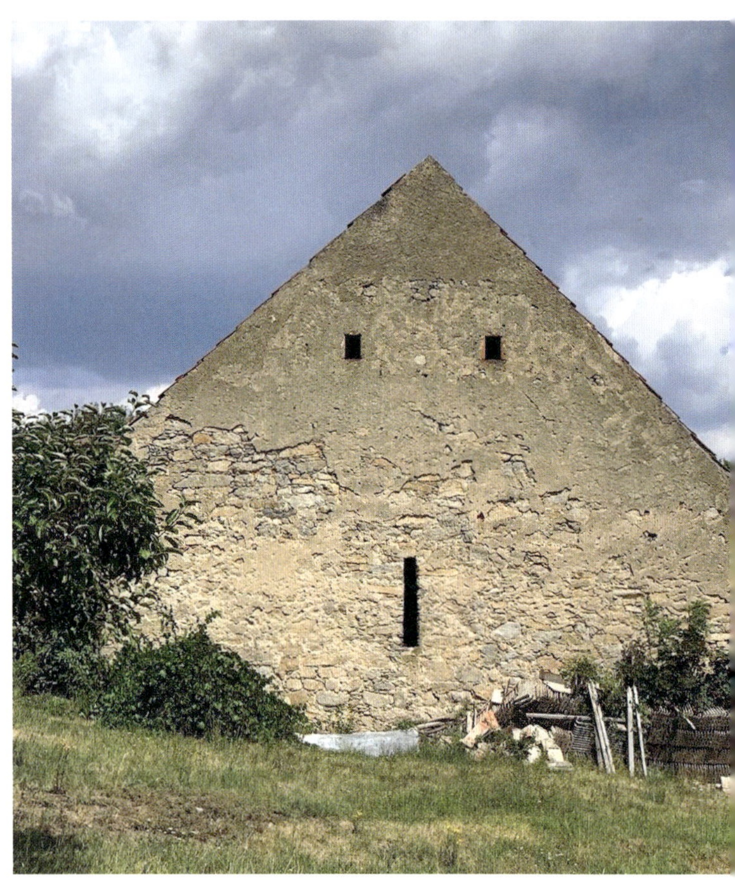

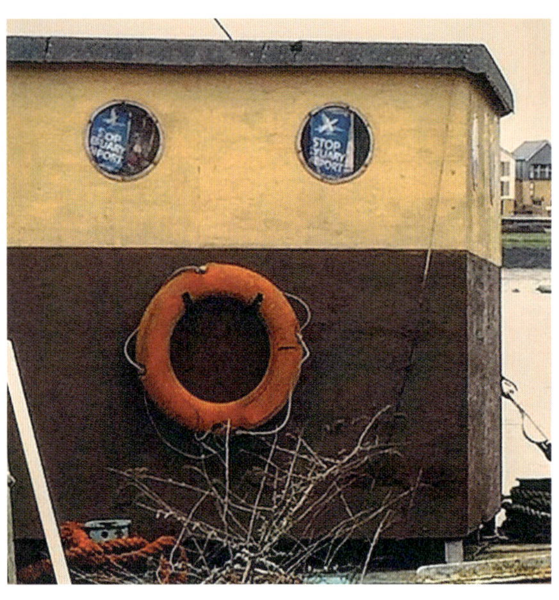
STOP

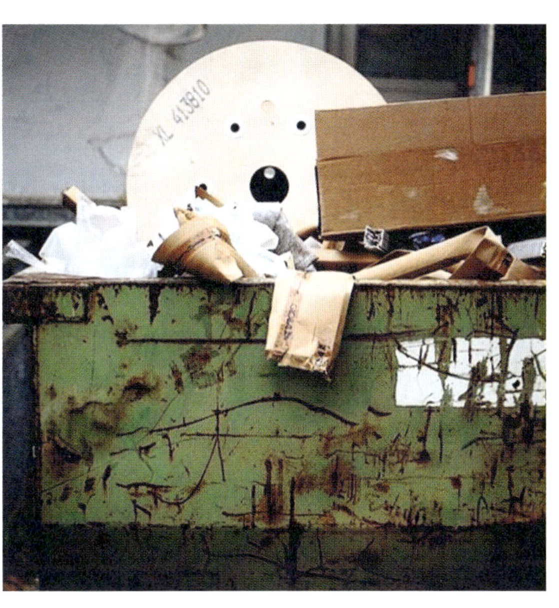
XL 413810

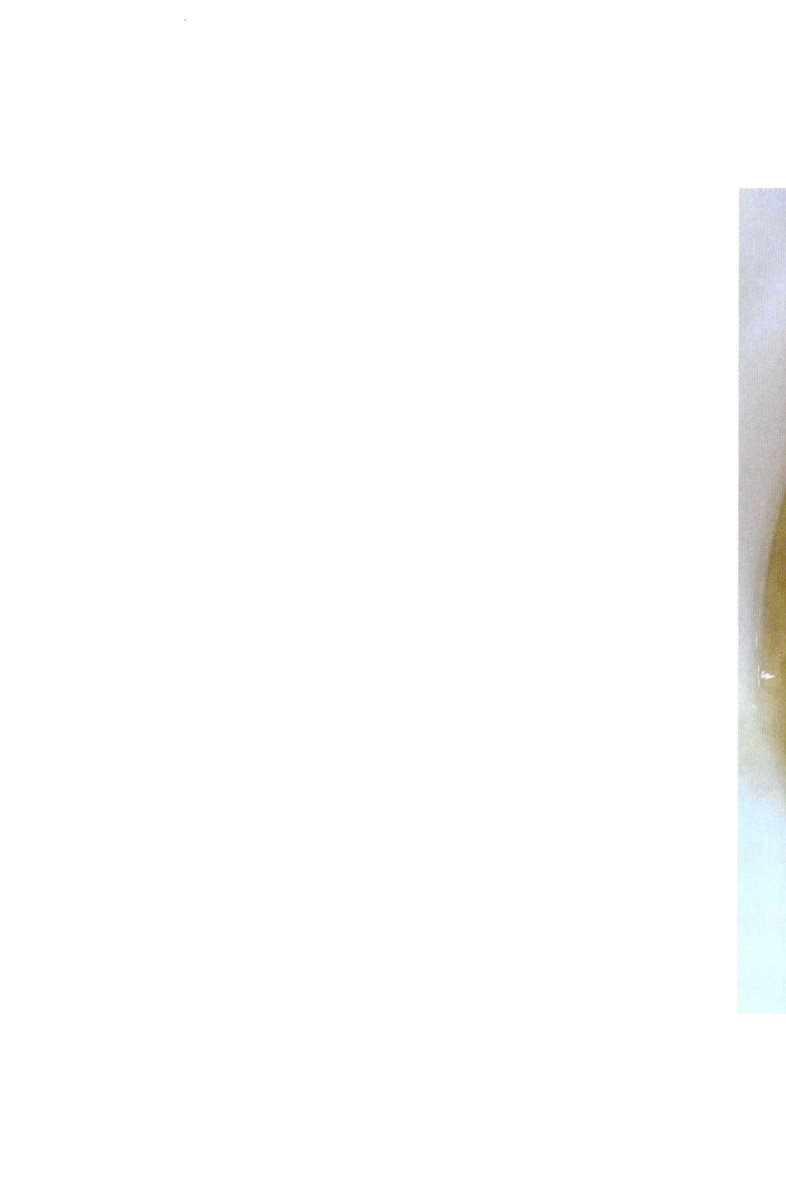

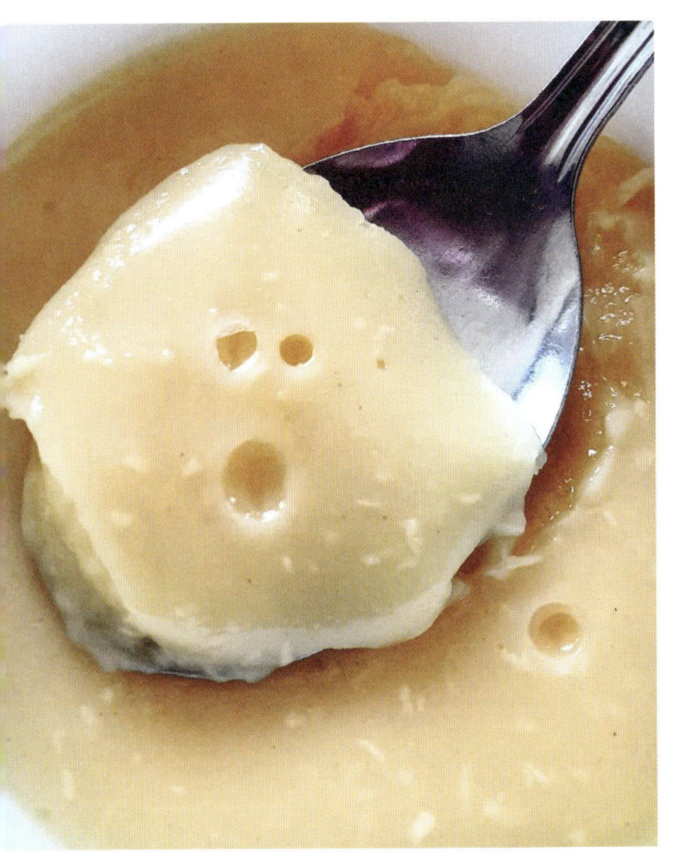

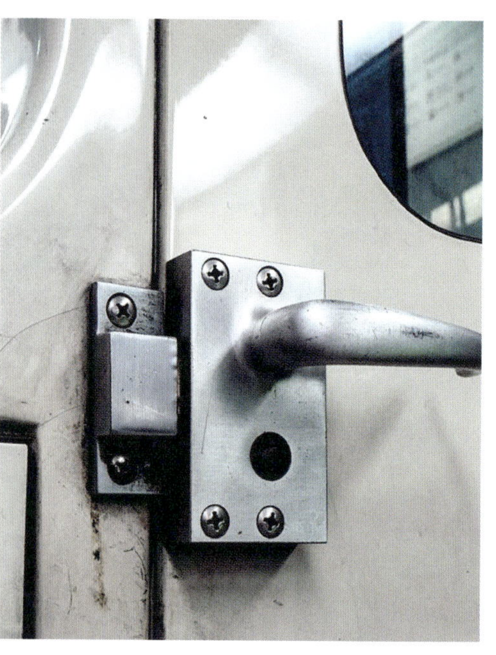

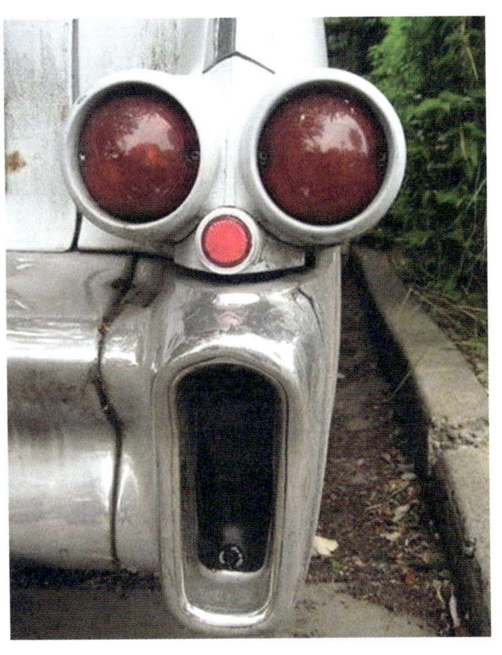

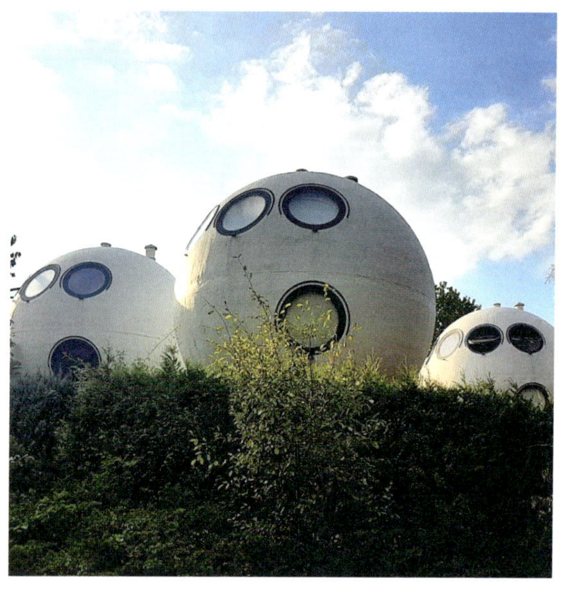

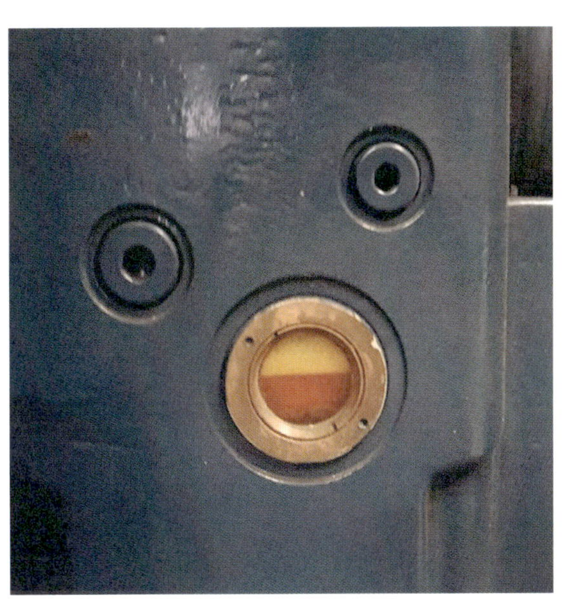

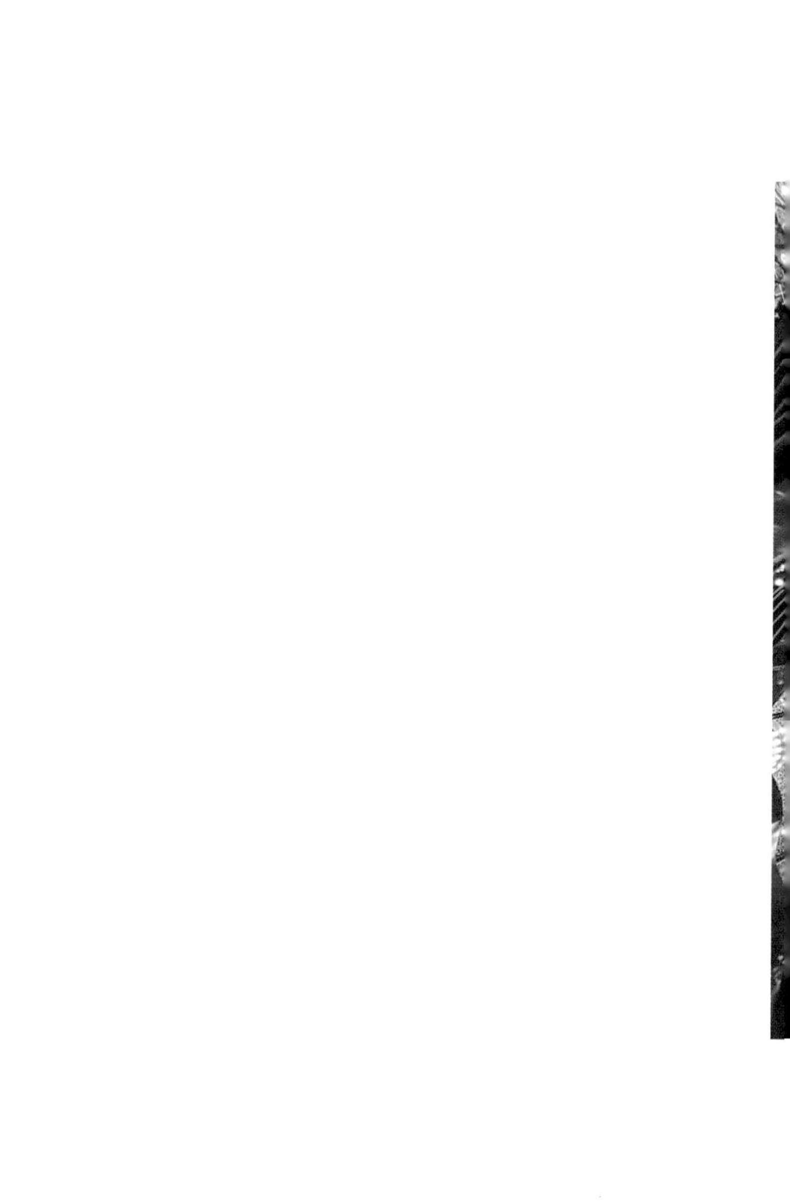

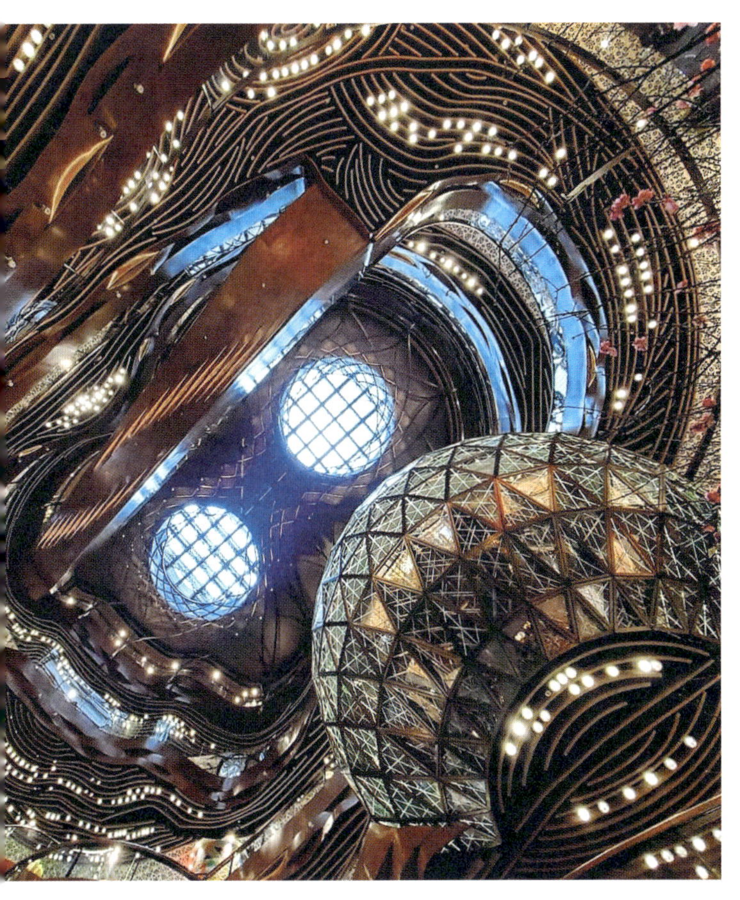

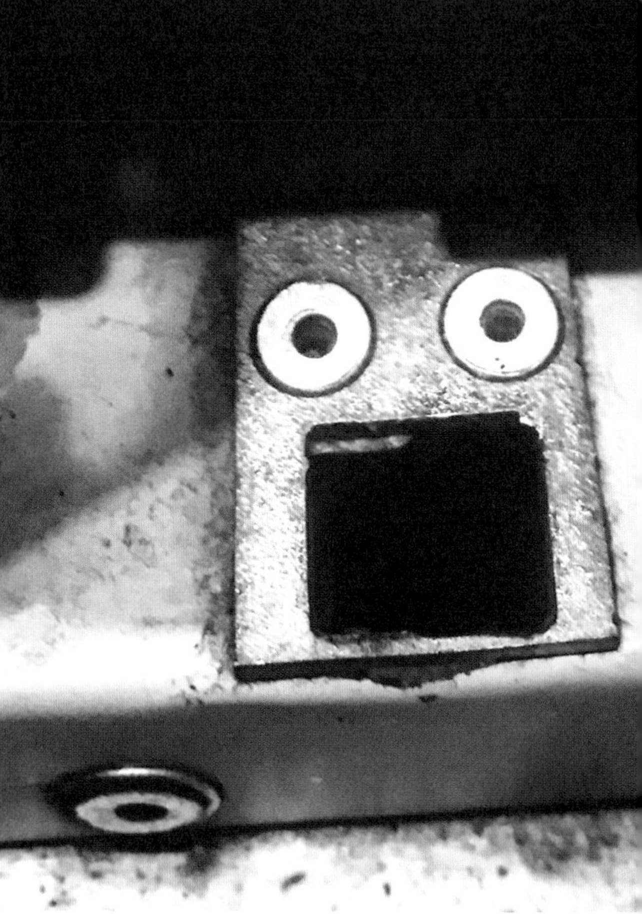

I SEE

FACES

TOO

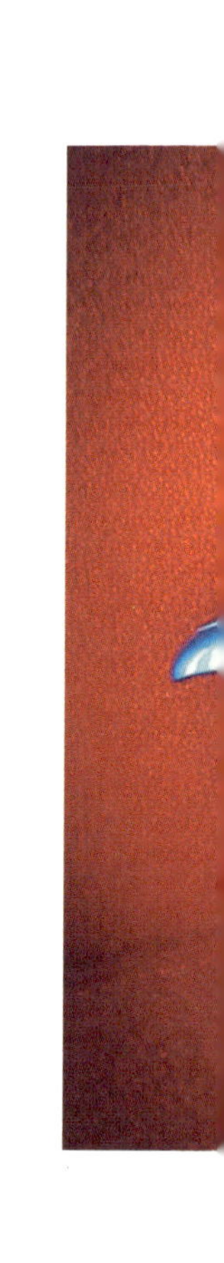

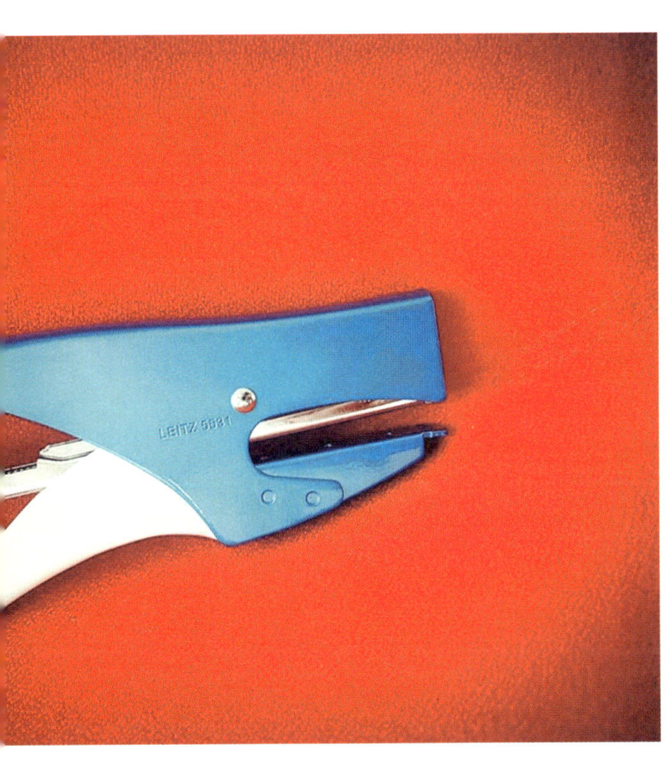
LEITZ

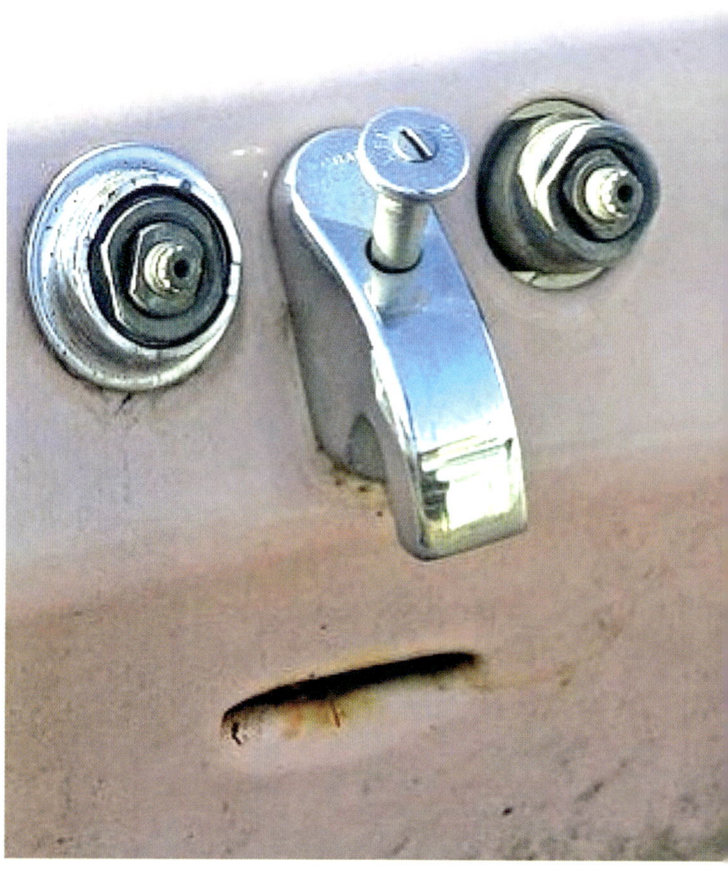

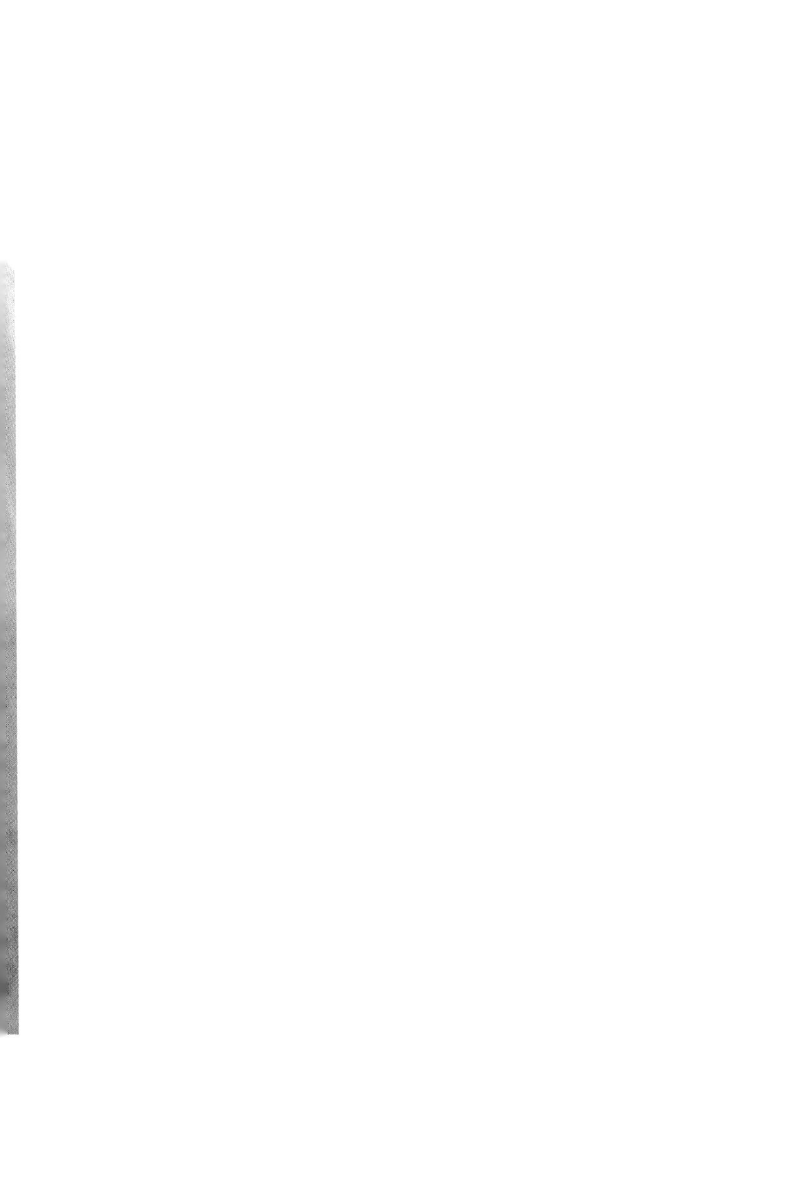

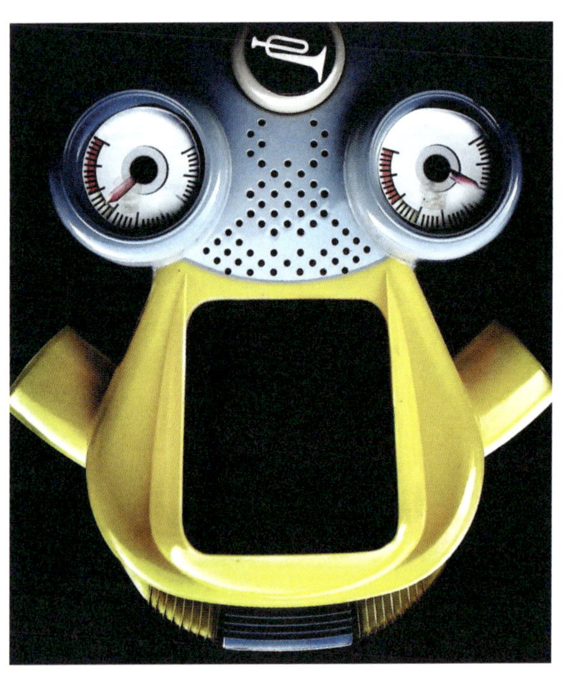

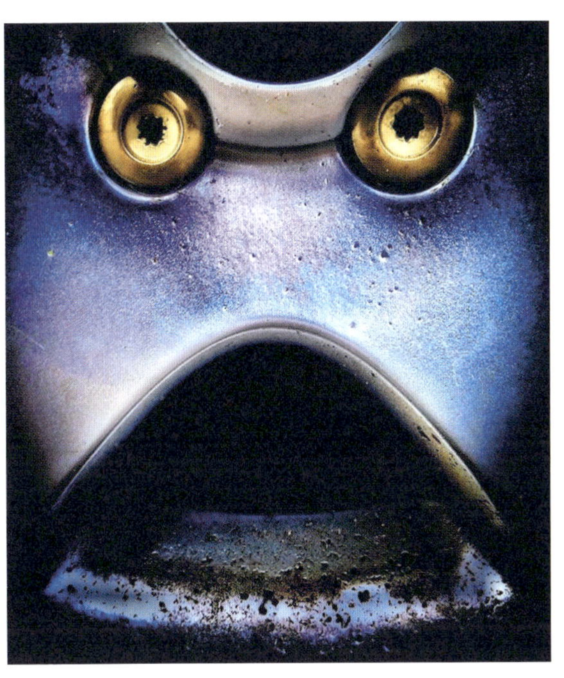

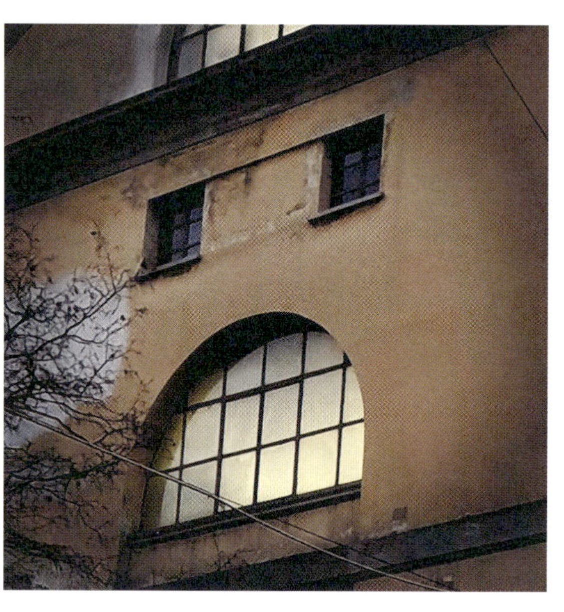

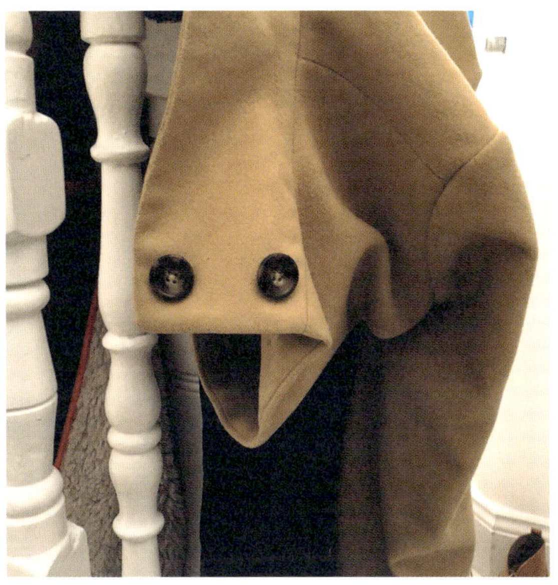

FACES

IN

BUILDINGS

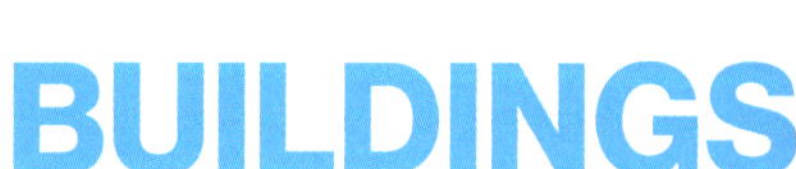

I SEE

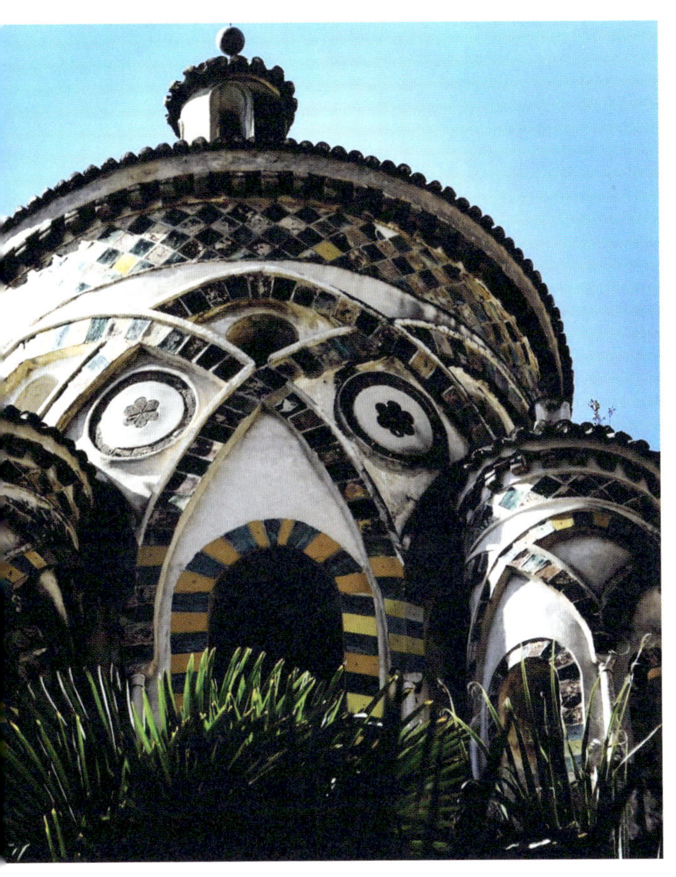

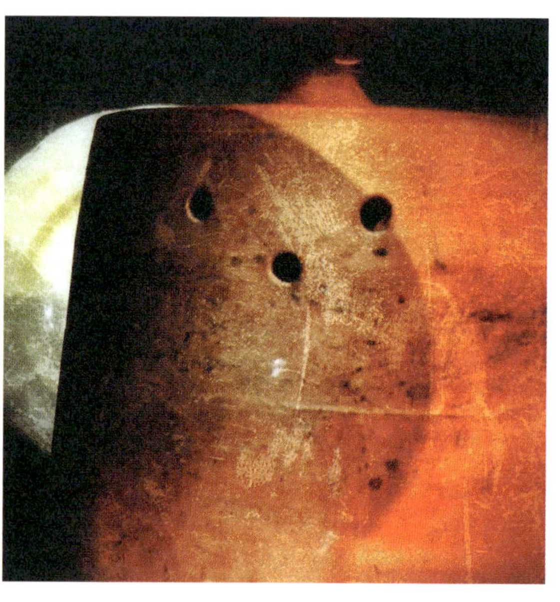

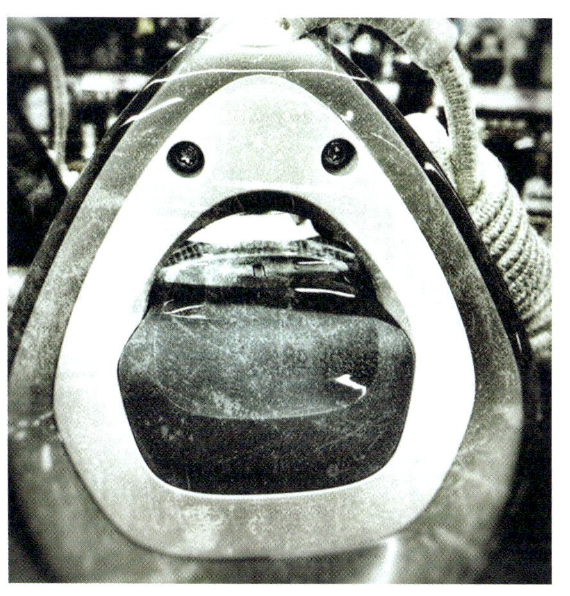

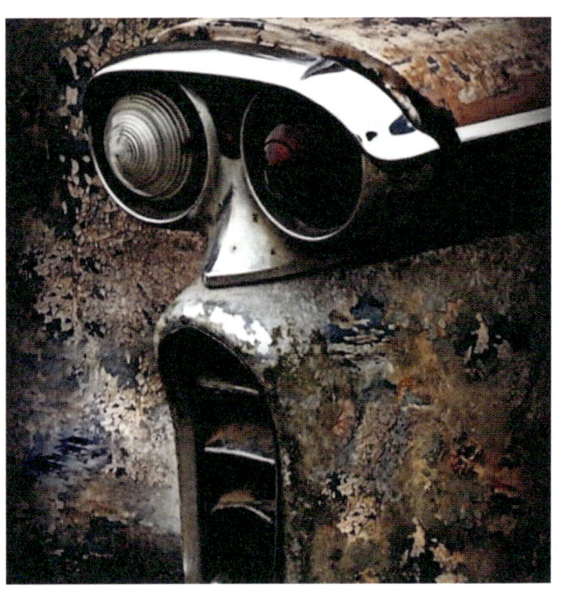

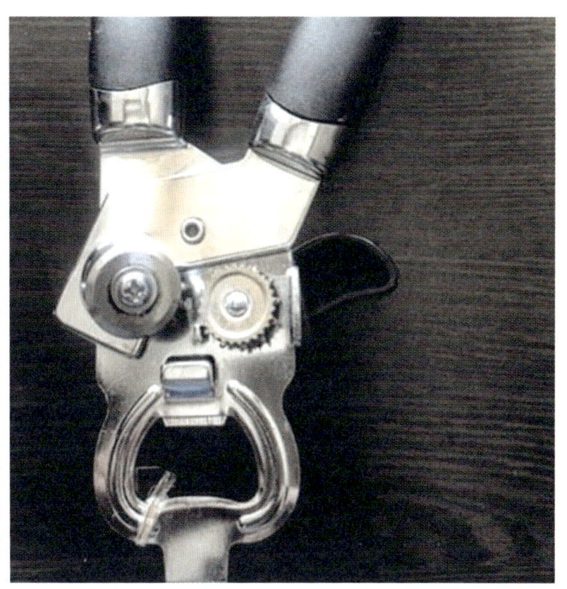

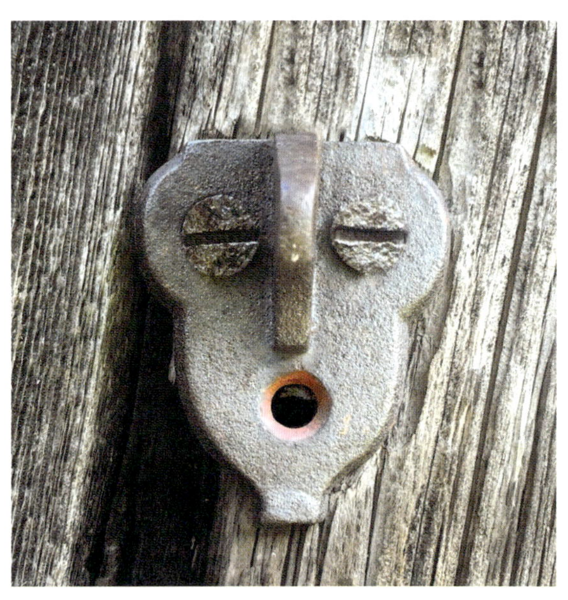

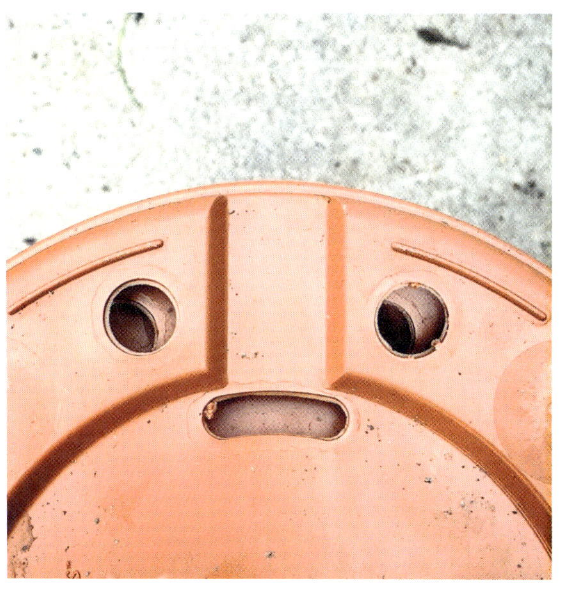

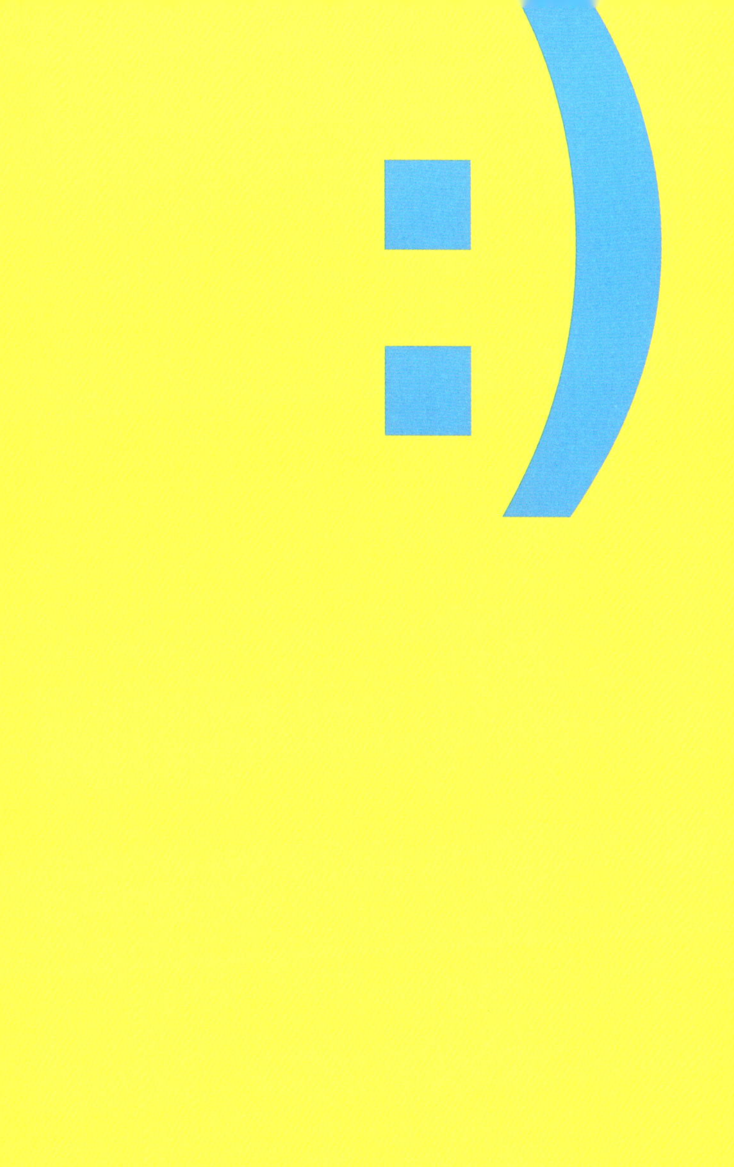

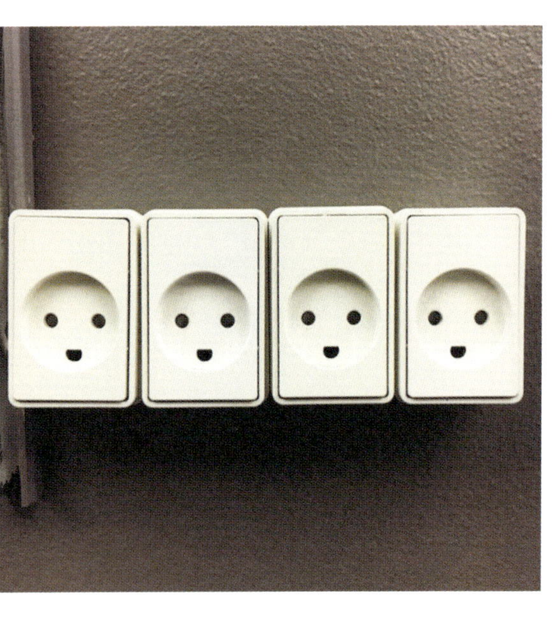

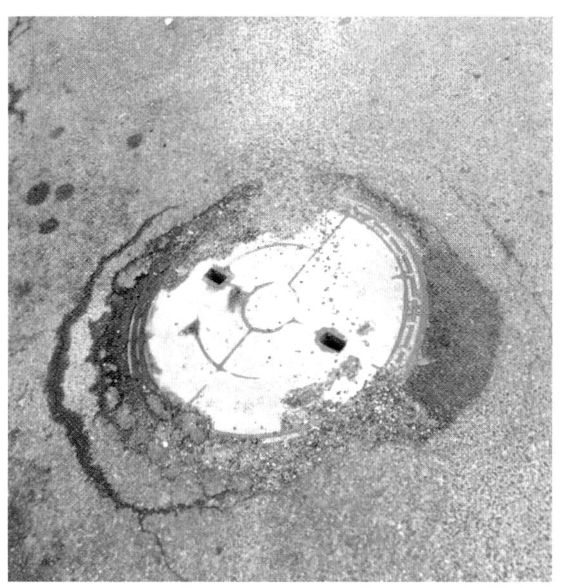

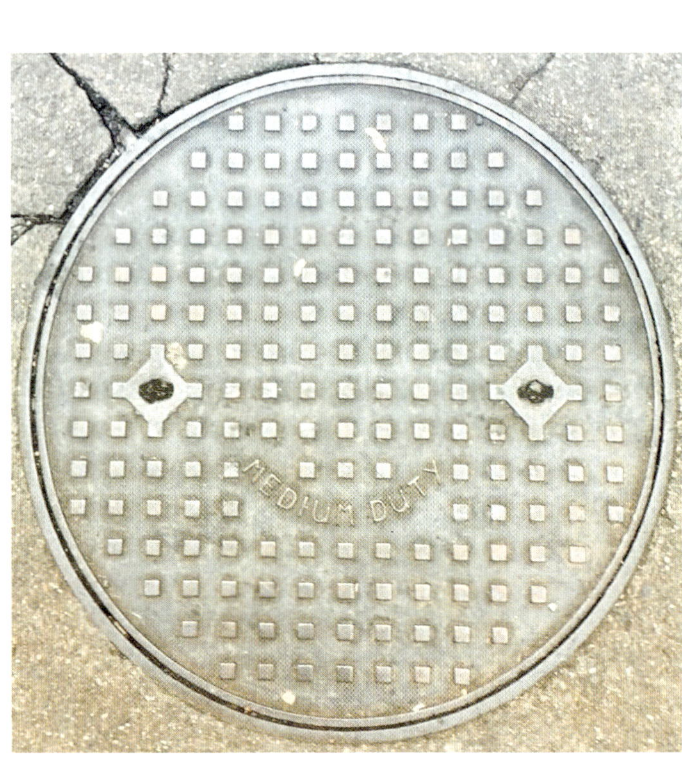
MEDIUM DUTY

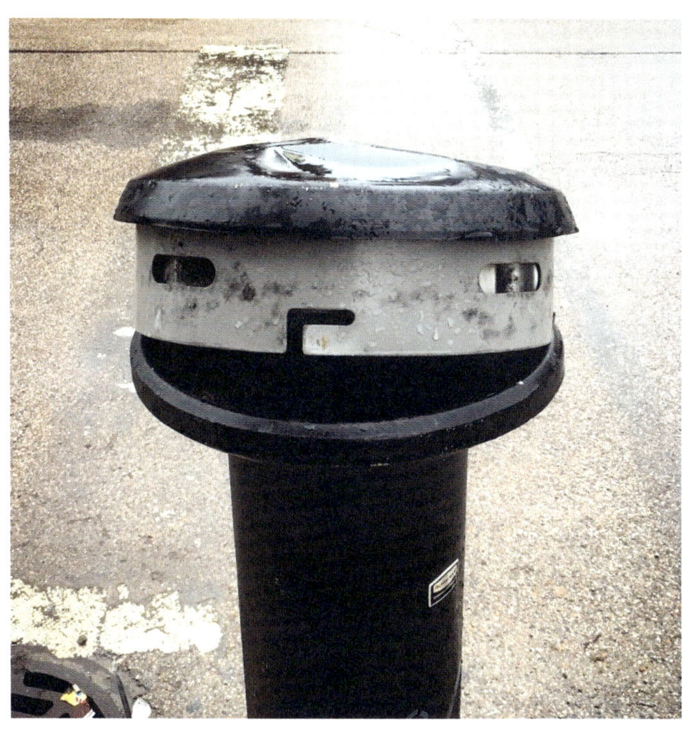

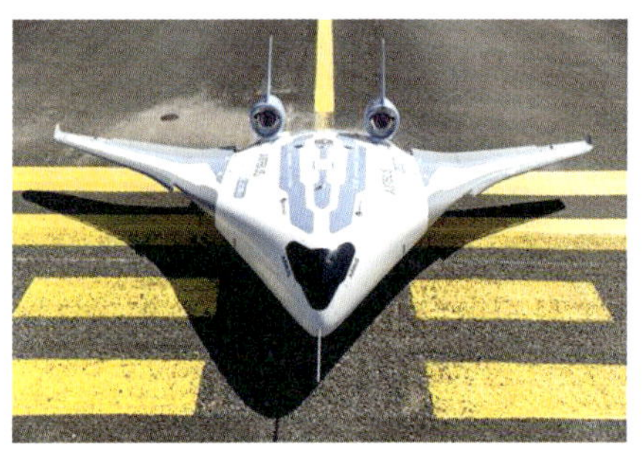

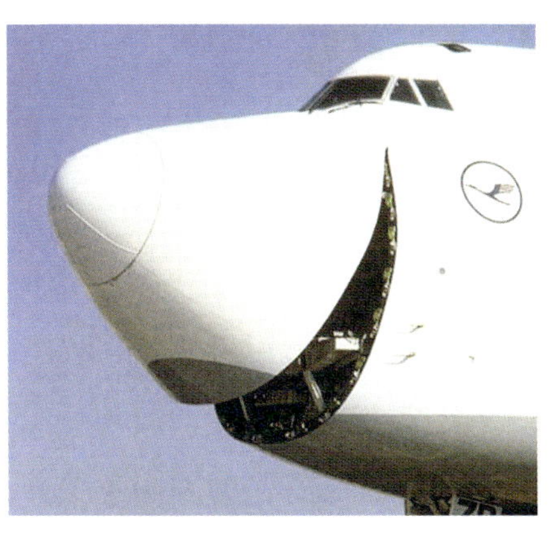

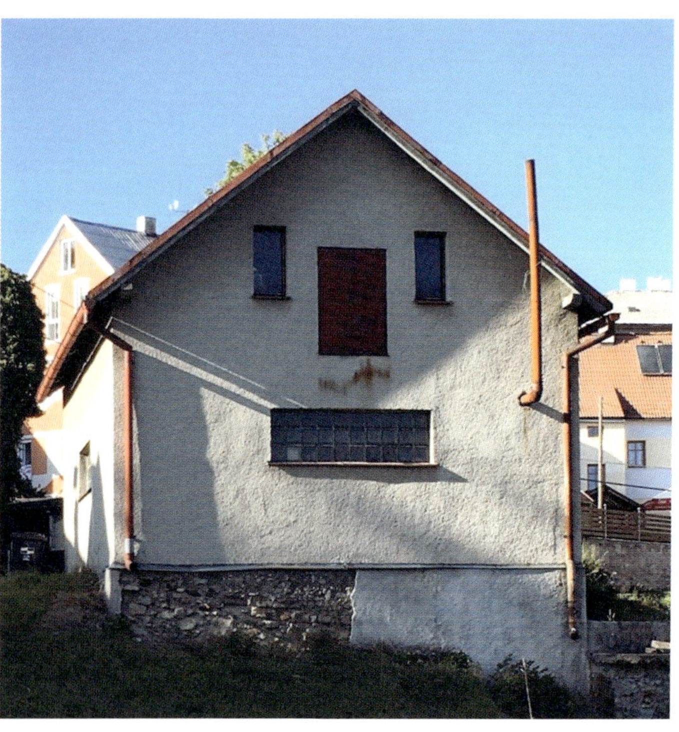

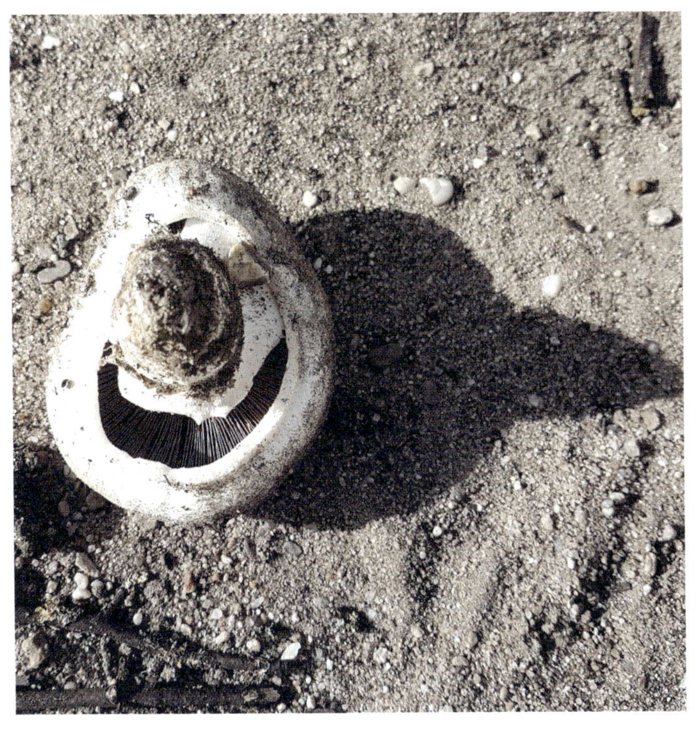

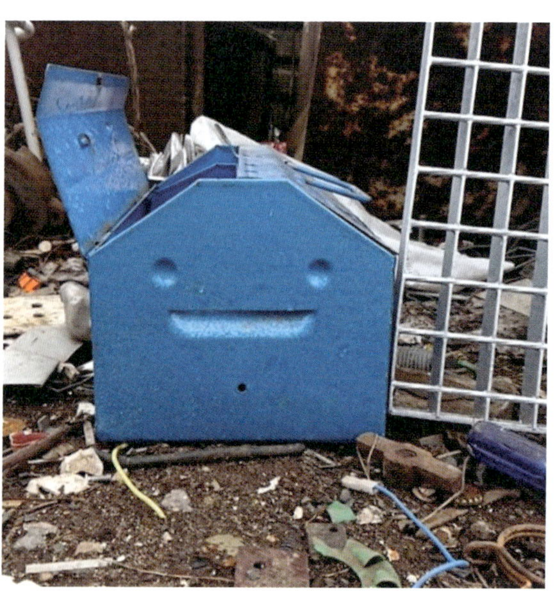

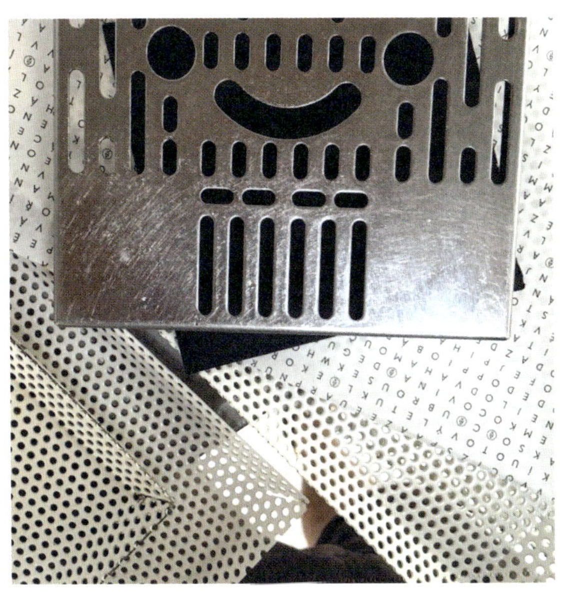

I SEE

FACES

IN THE

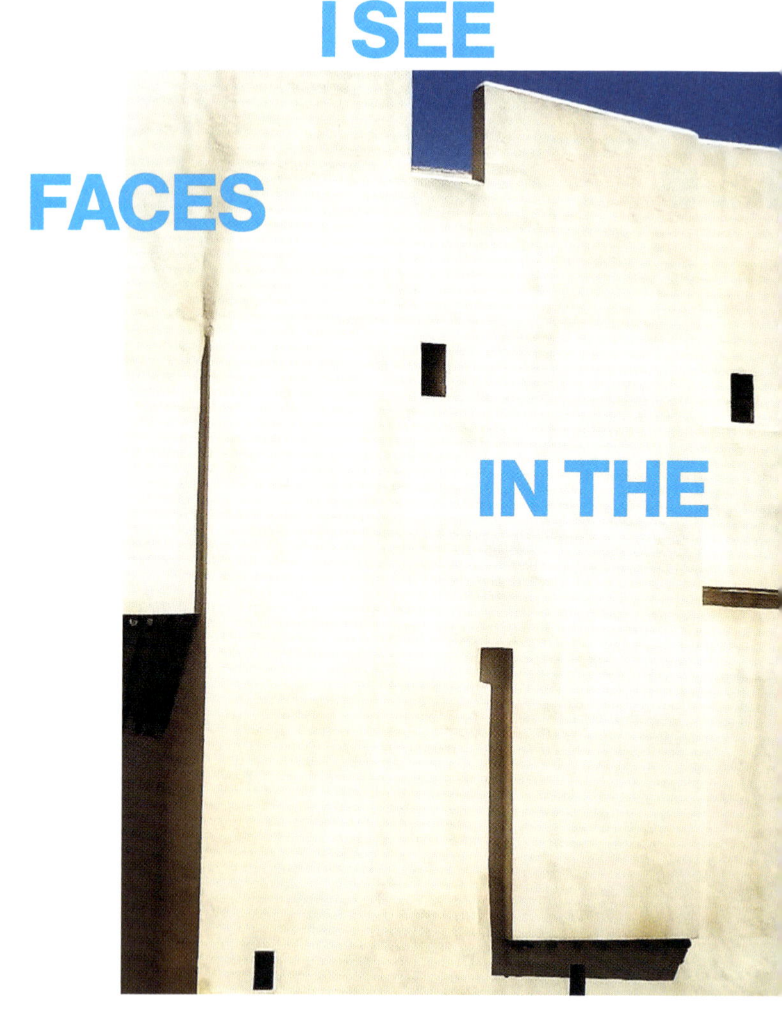

STRANGEST

PLACES

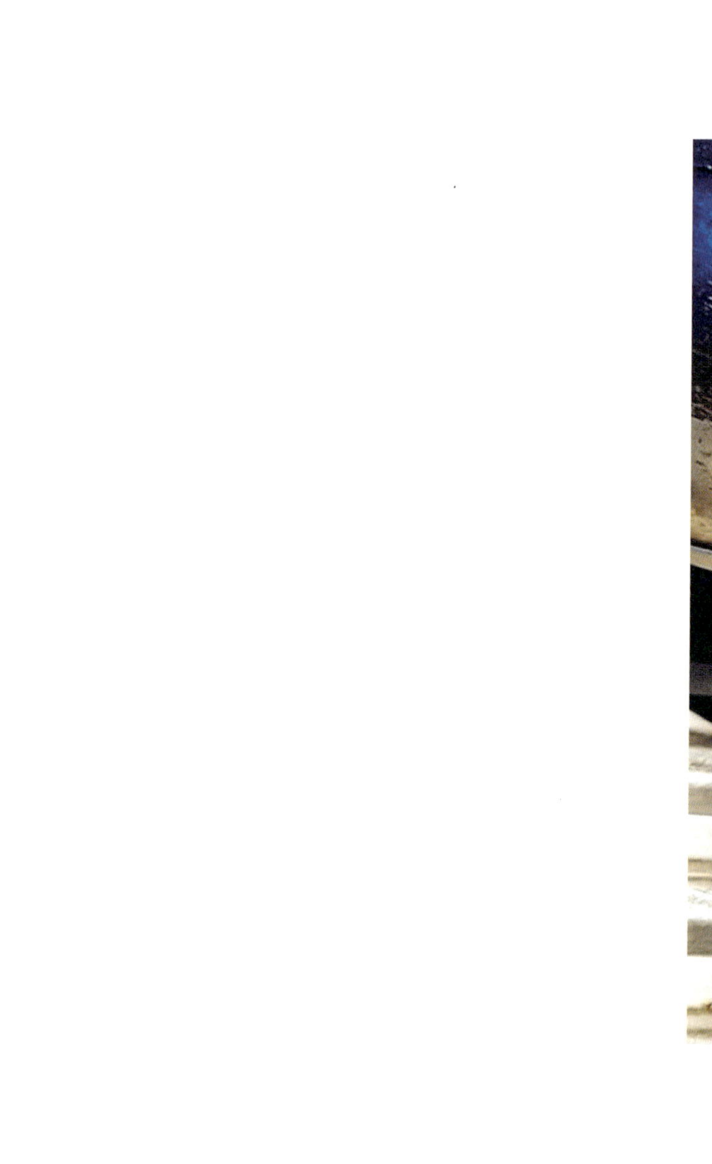

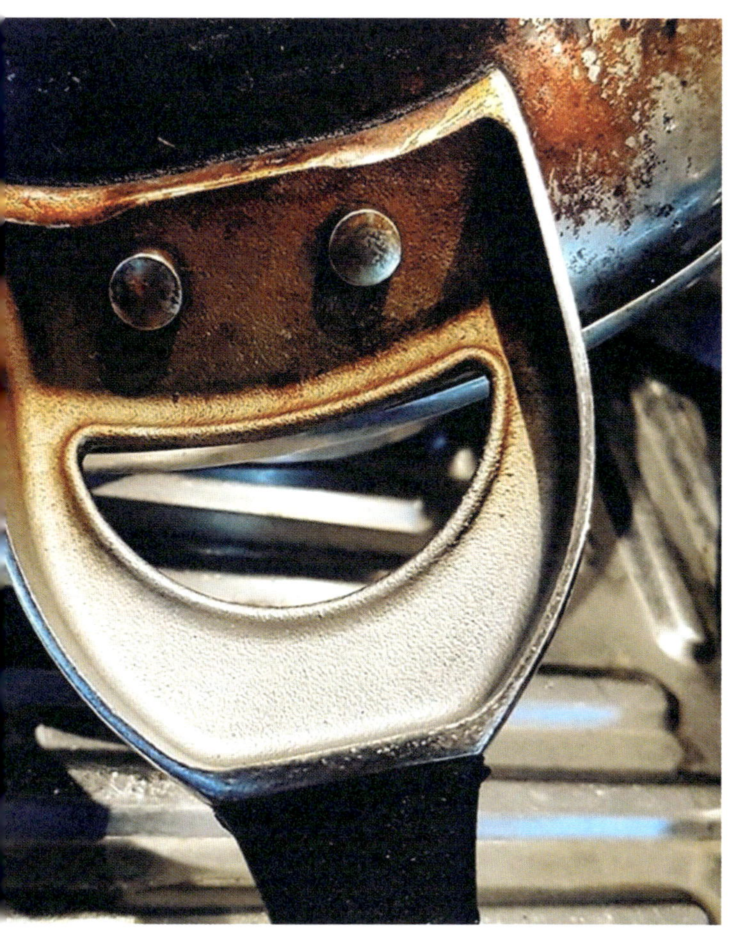

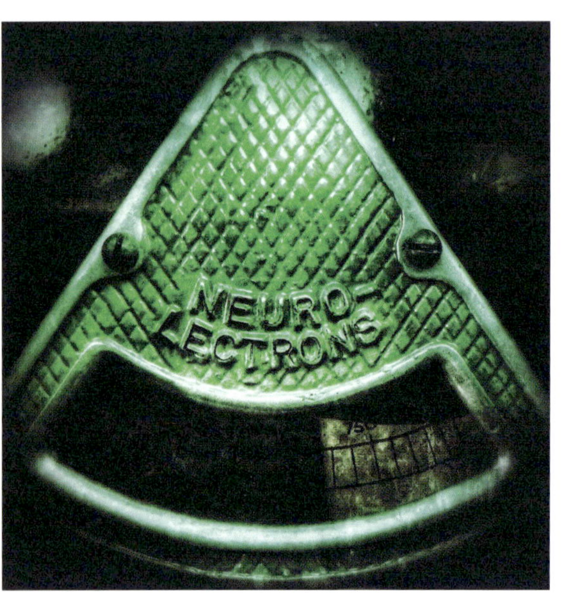
NEURO-
LECTRONS

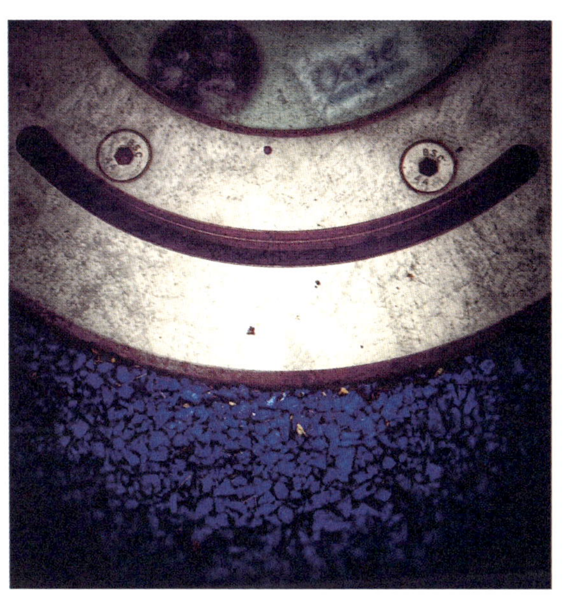

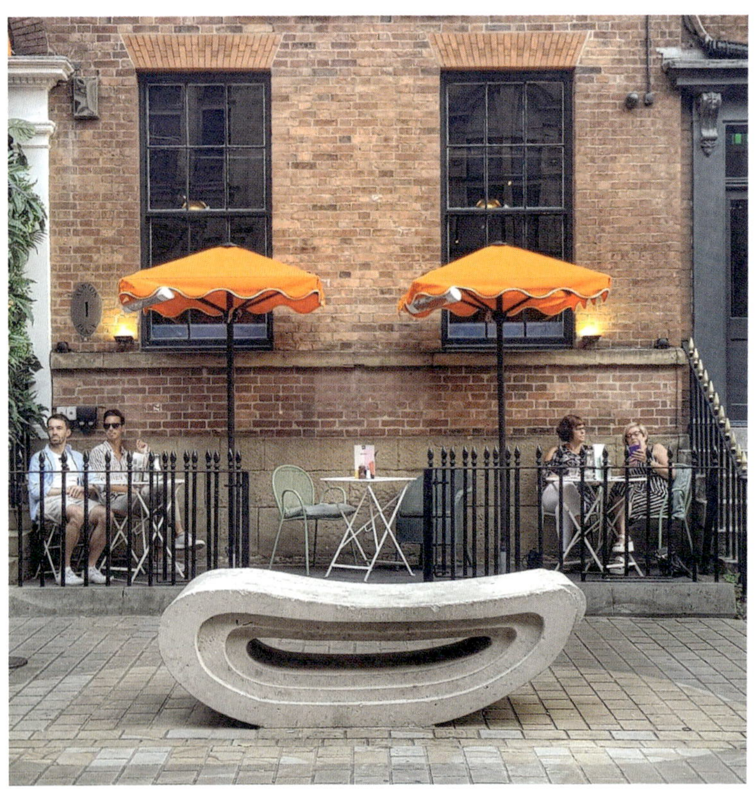

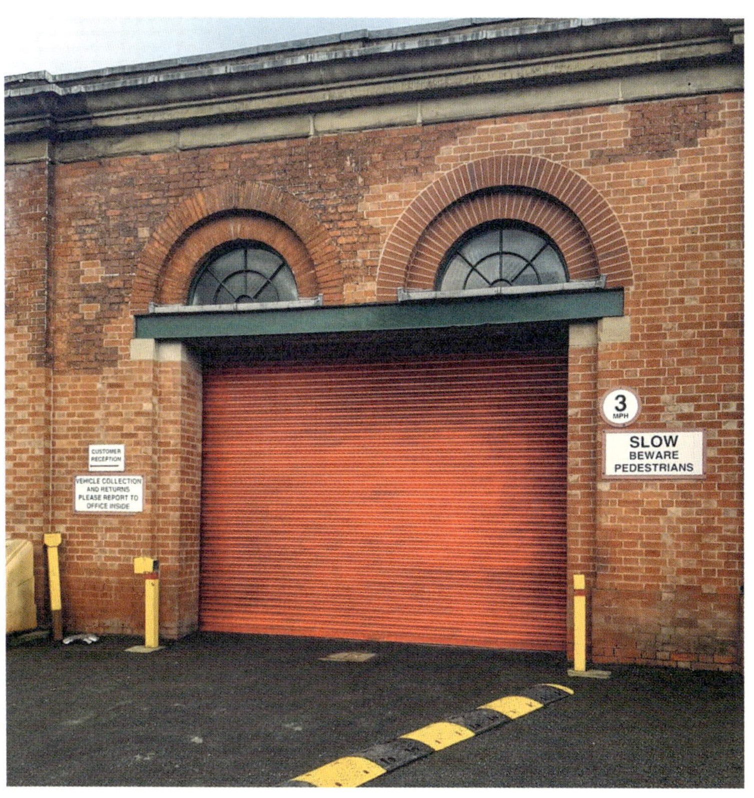
CUSTOMER
RECEPTION
VEHICLE COLLECTION
AND RETURNS
PLEASE REPORT TO
OFFICE INSIDE
3
MPH
SLOW
BEWARE
PEDESTRIANS

I SEE

FACES

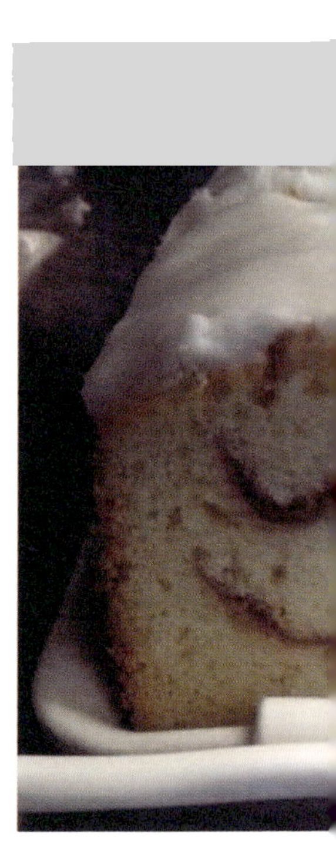

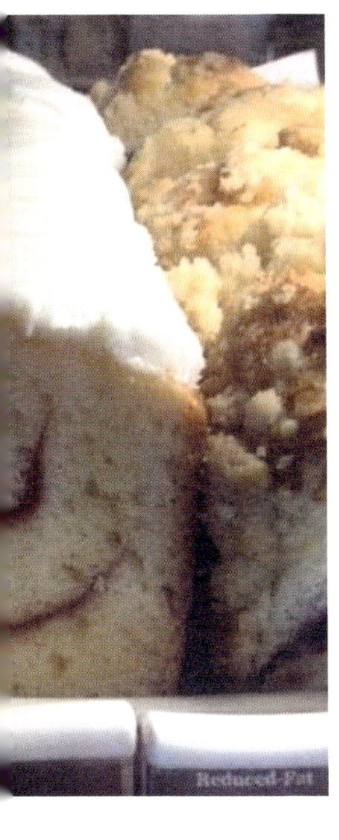

IN

FOOD

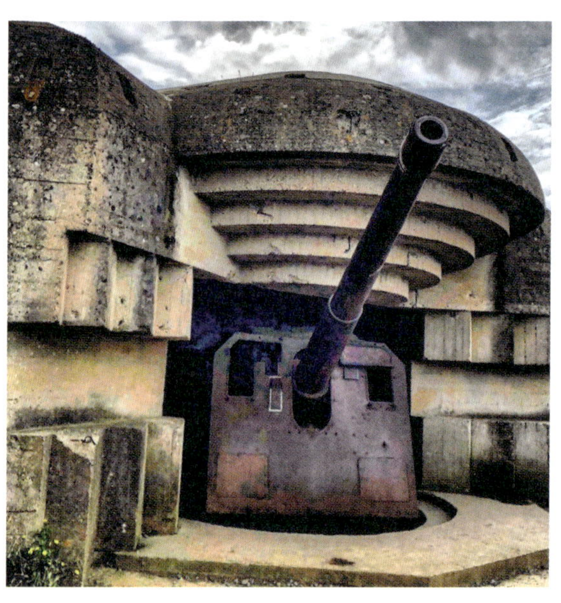

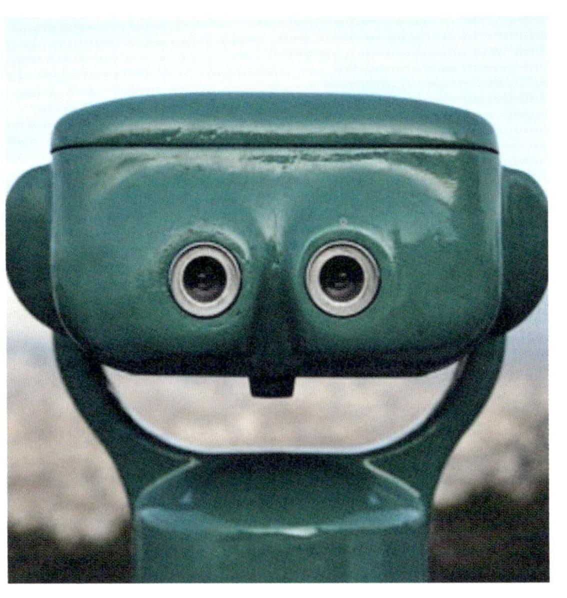

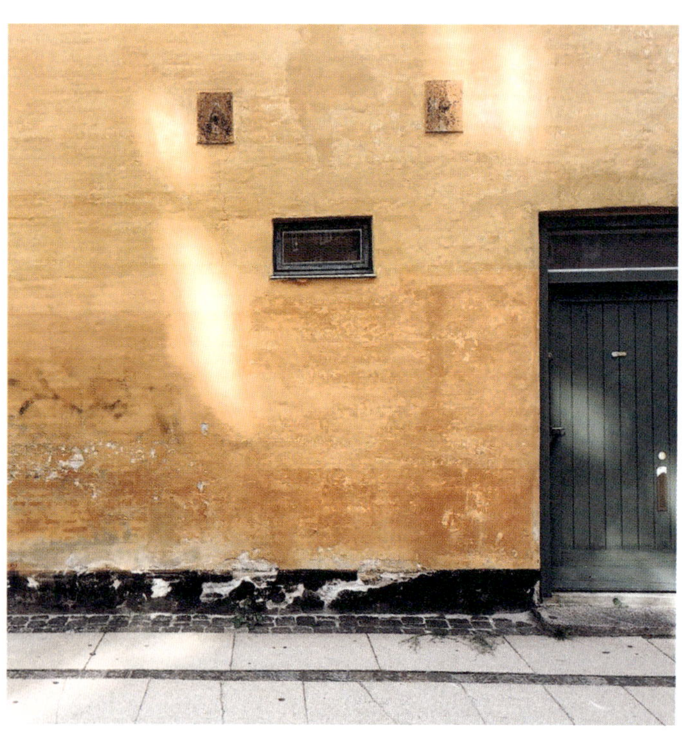

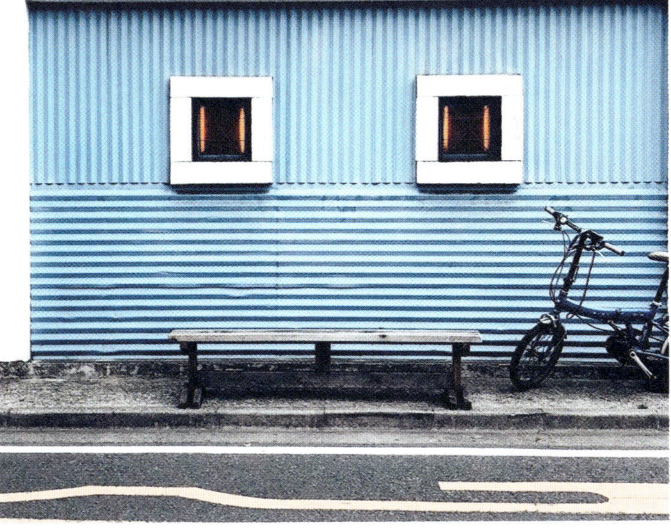

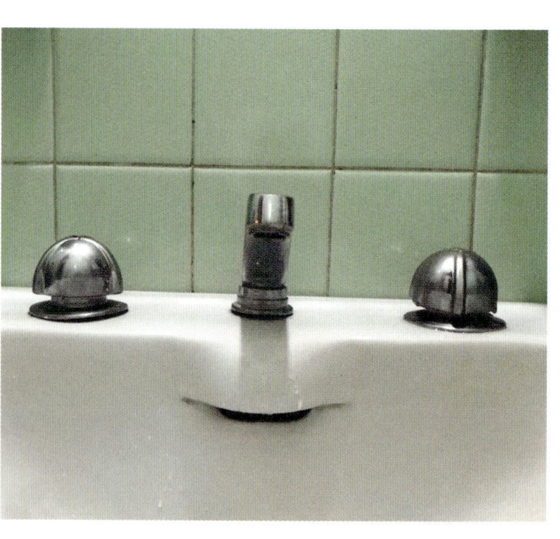

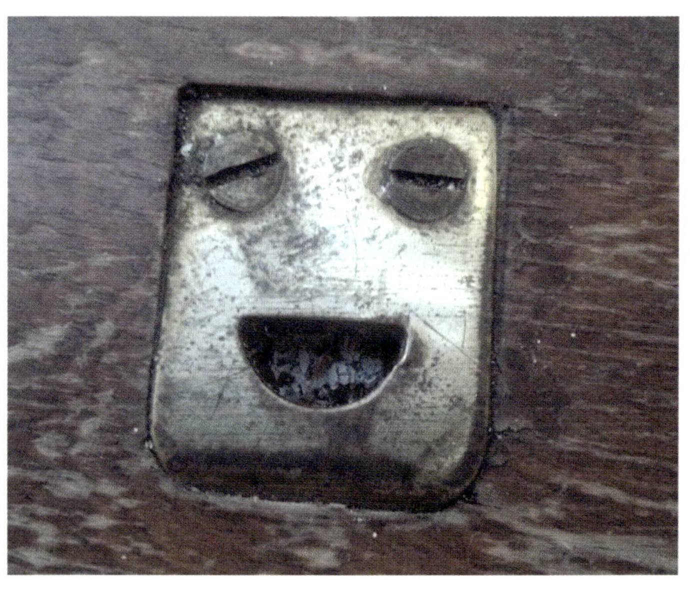

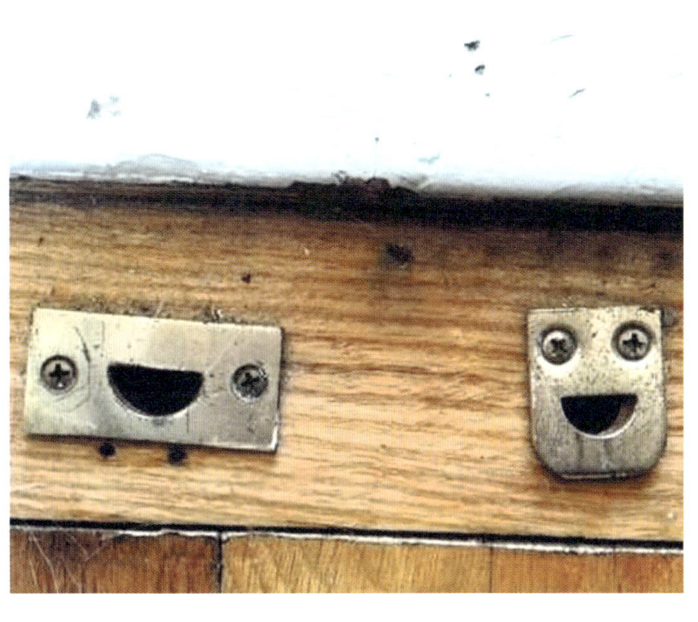

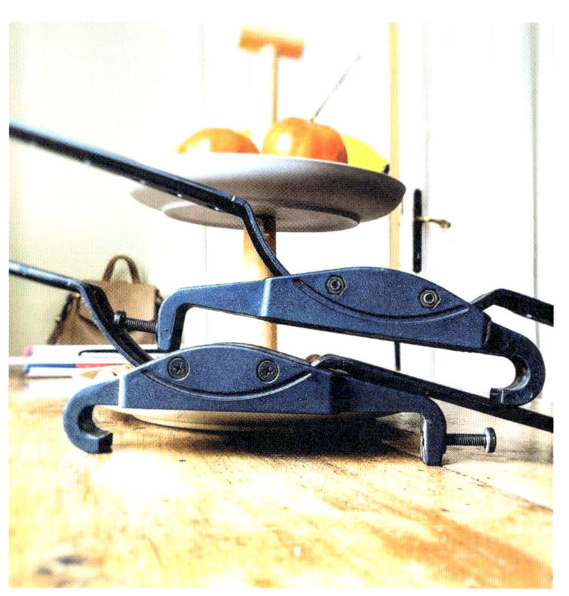

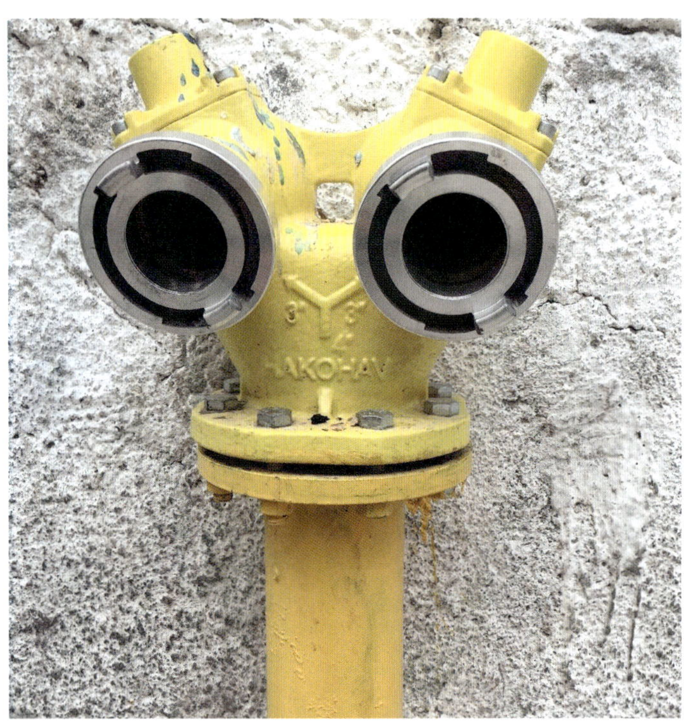

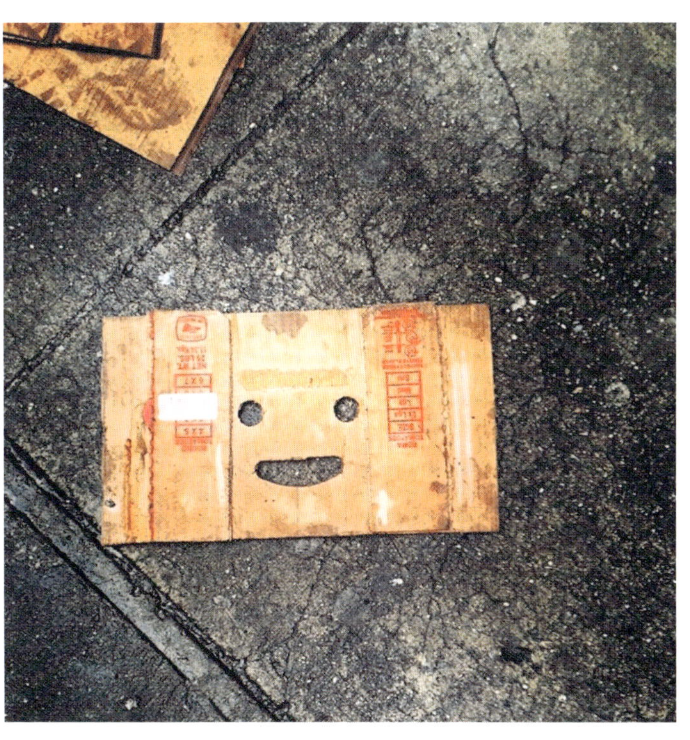

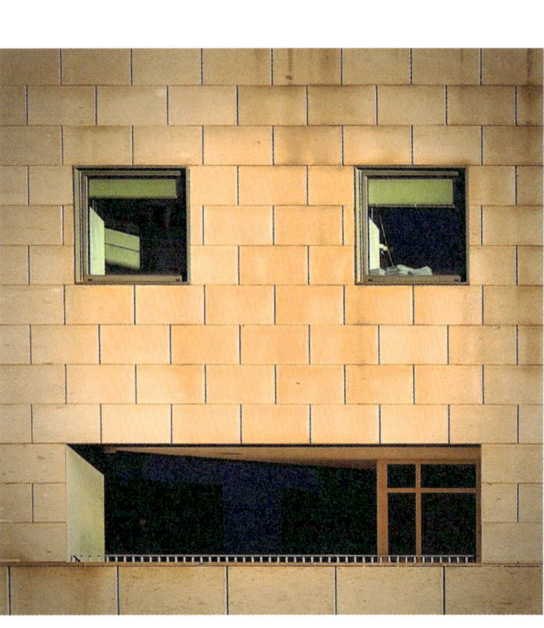

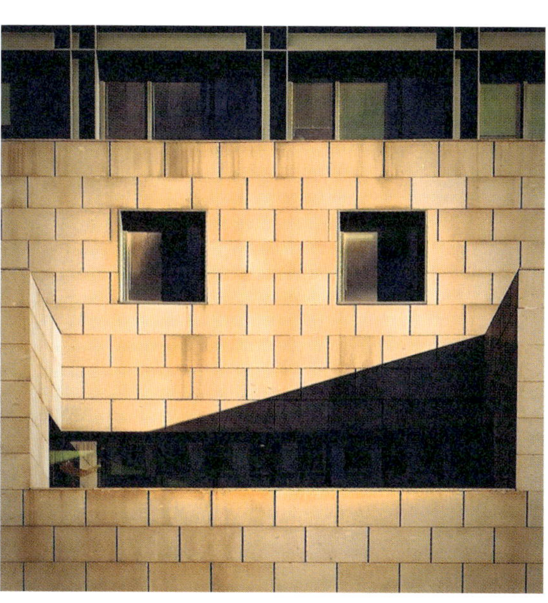

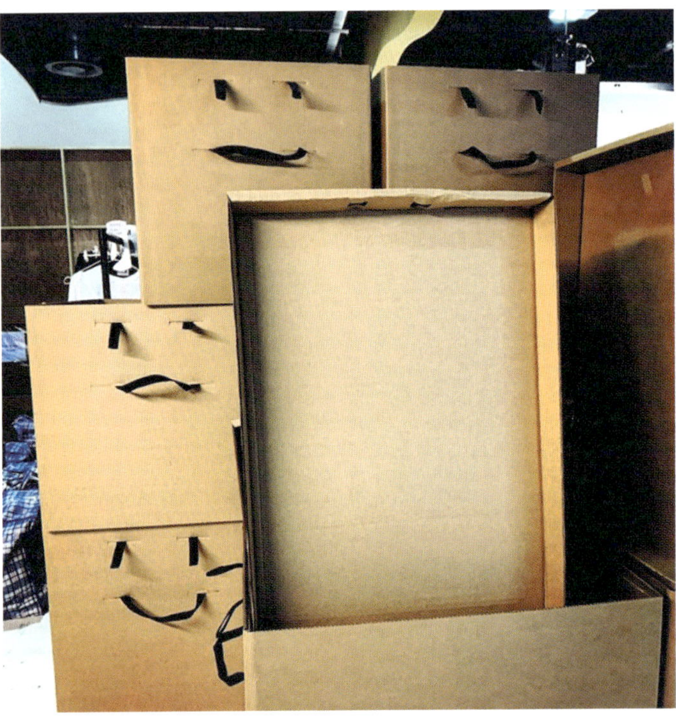

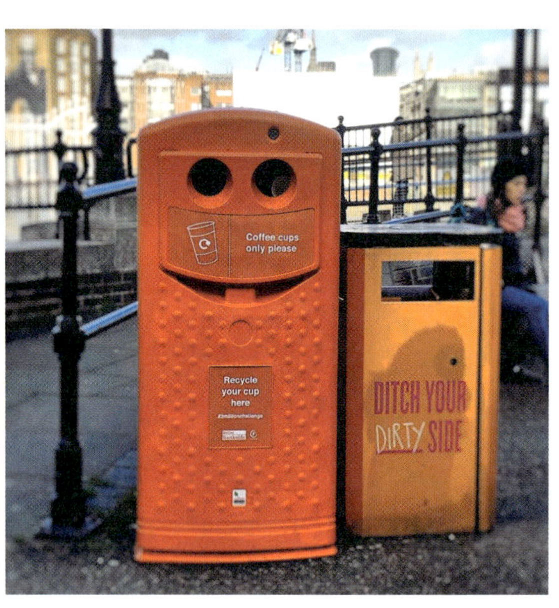
Coffee cups
only please
Recycle
your cup
here
DITCH YOUR
DIRTY SIDE

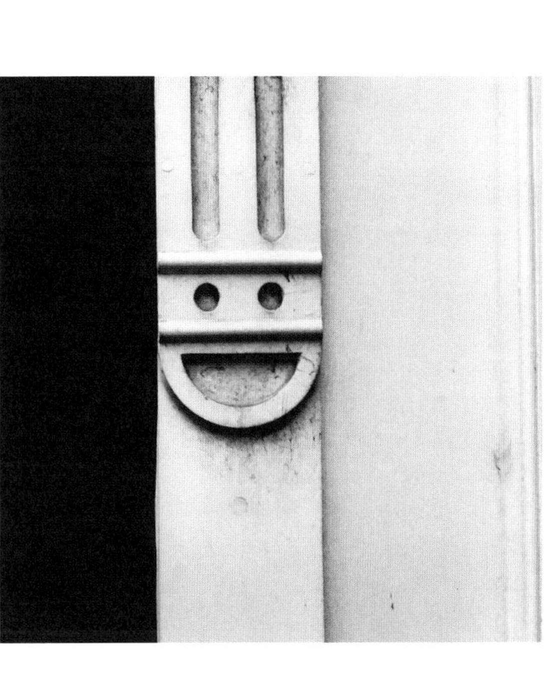

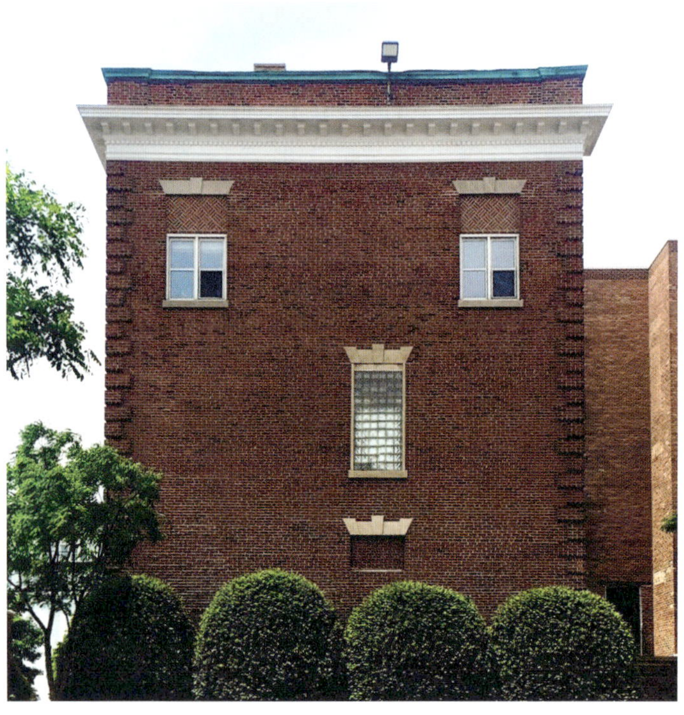

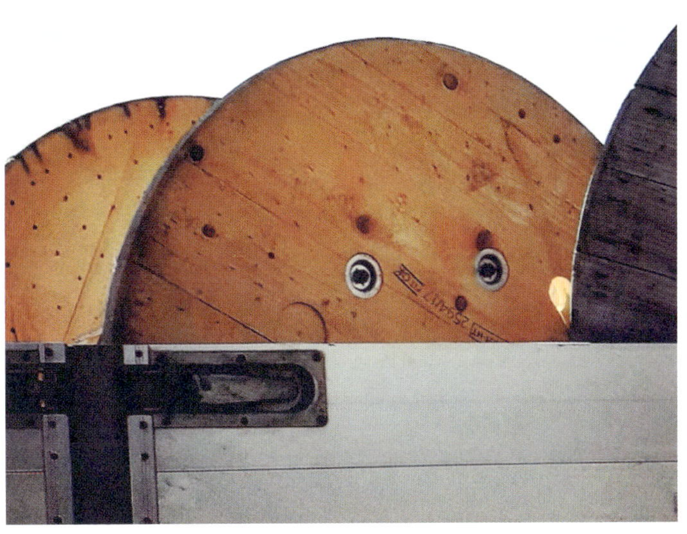

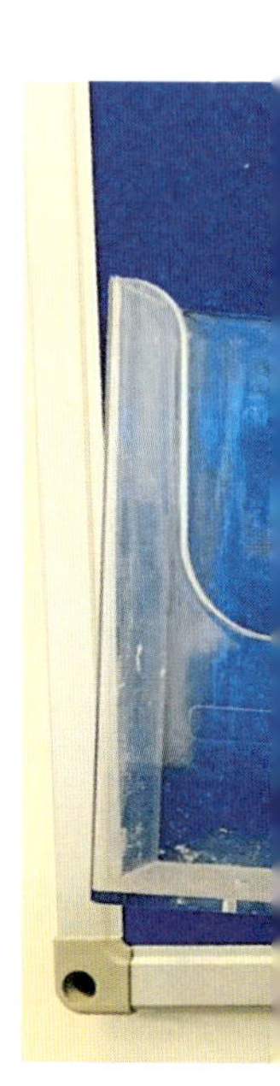

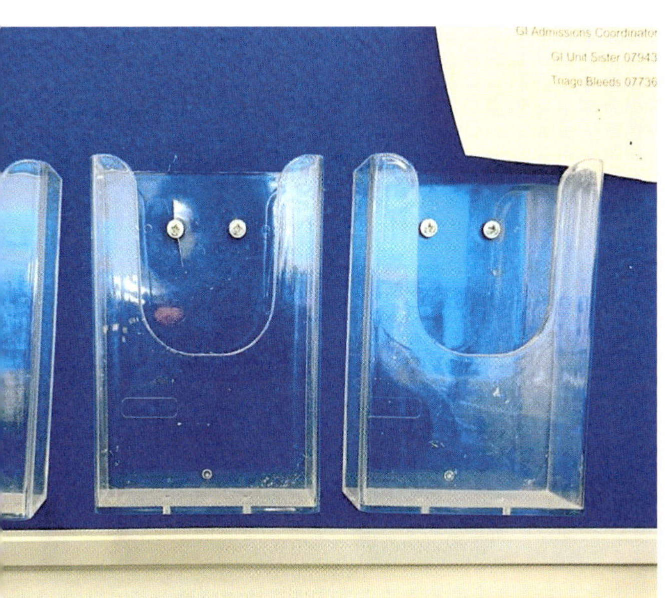
GI Admissions Coordinator
GI Unit Sister 07943
Triage Bleeds 07736

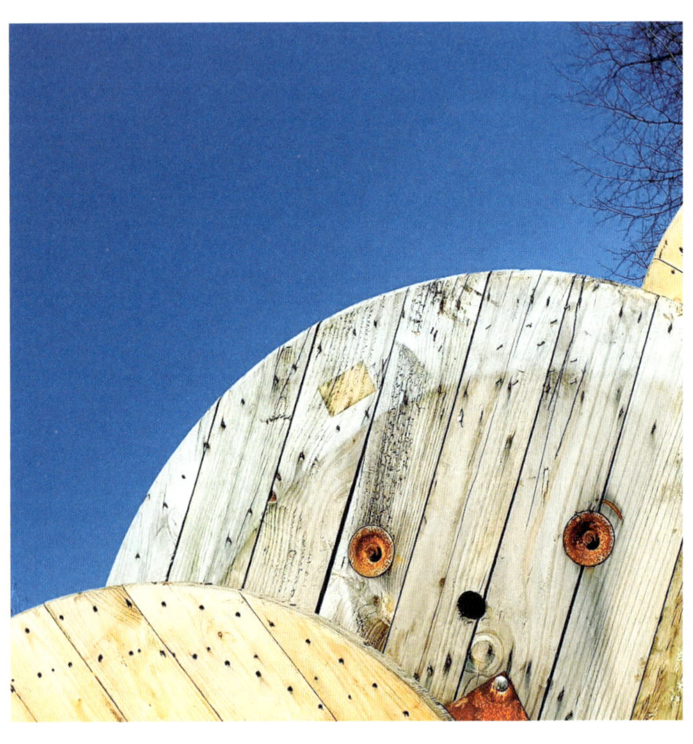

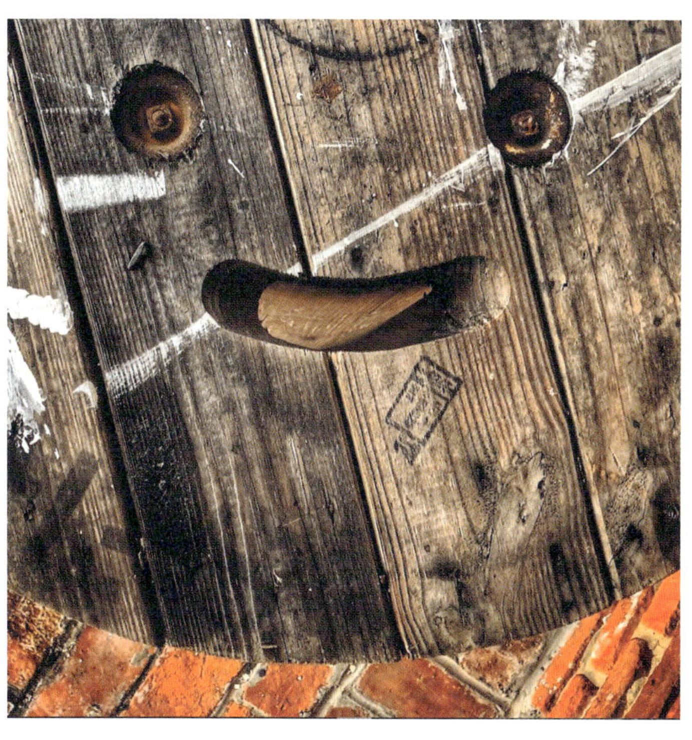

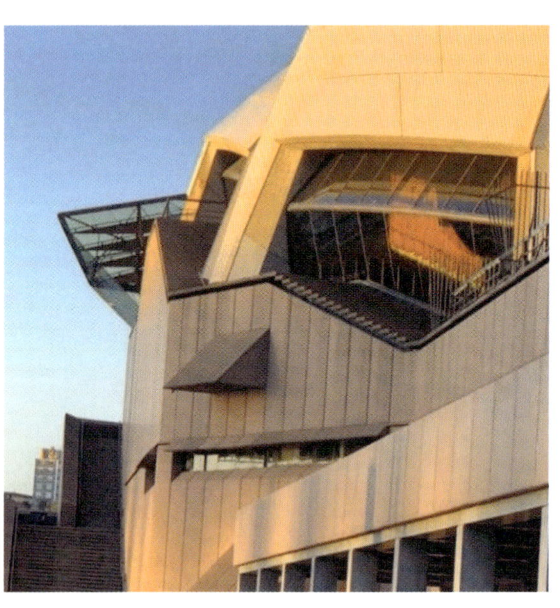

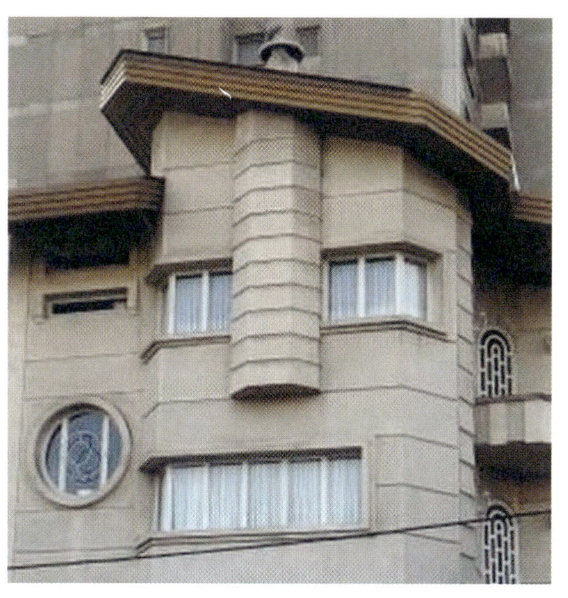

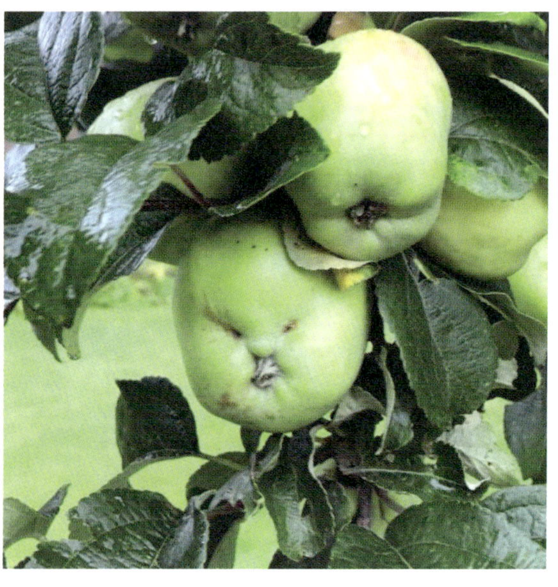

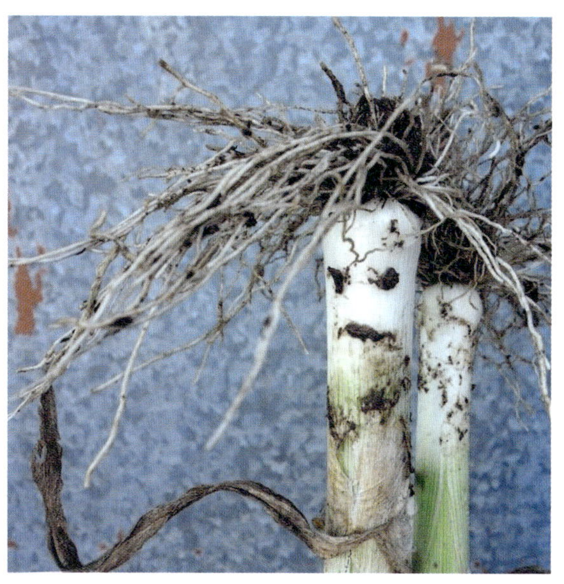

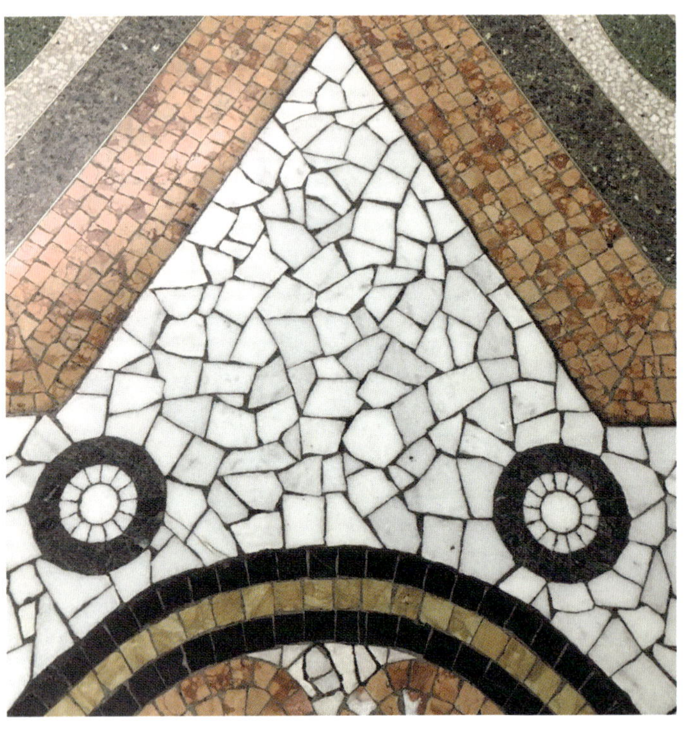

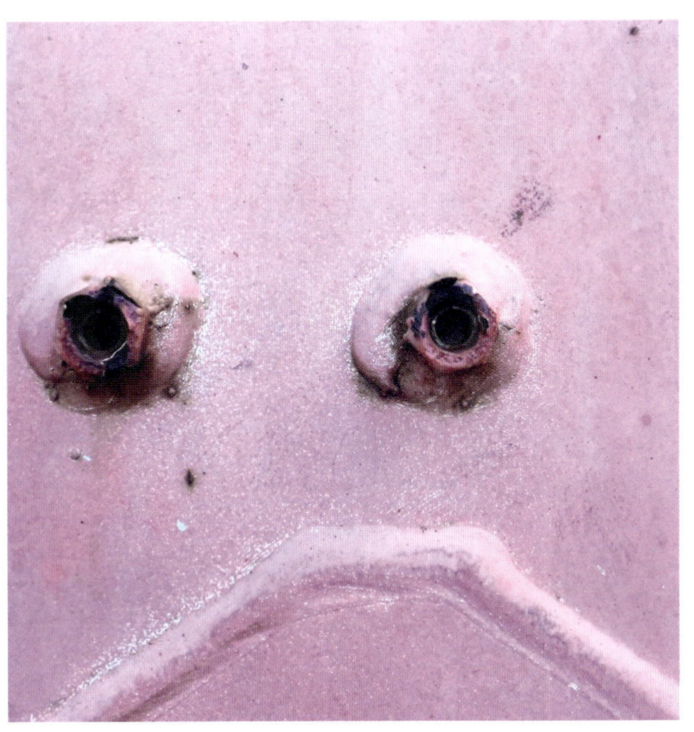

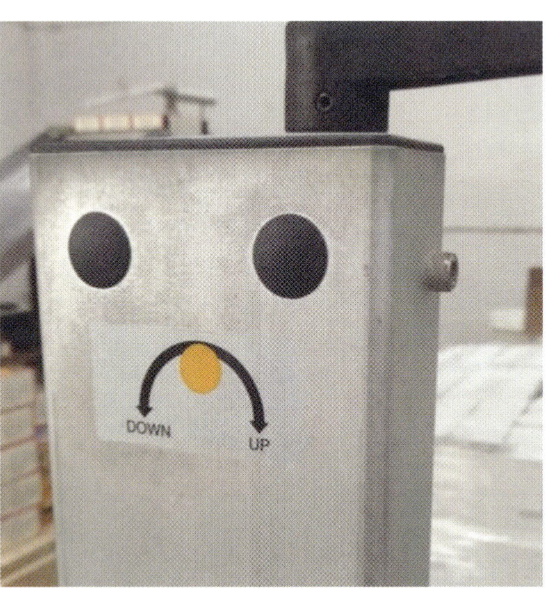
DOWN
UP

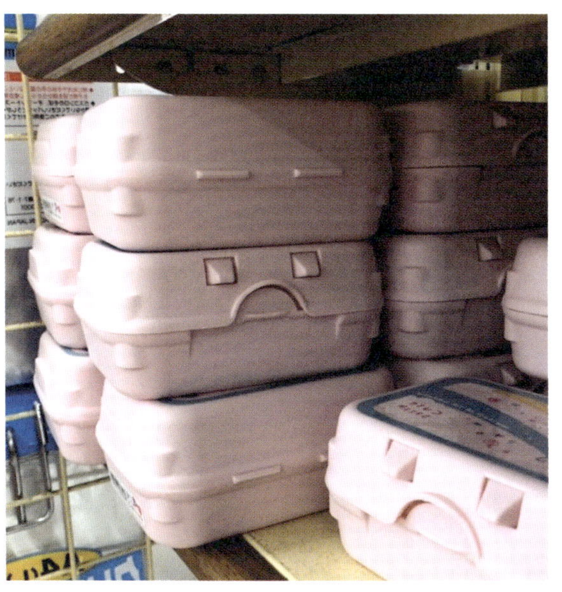

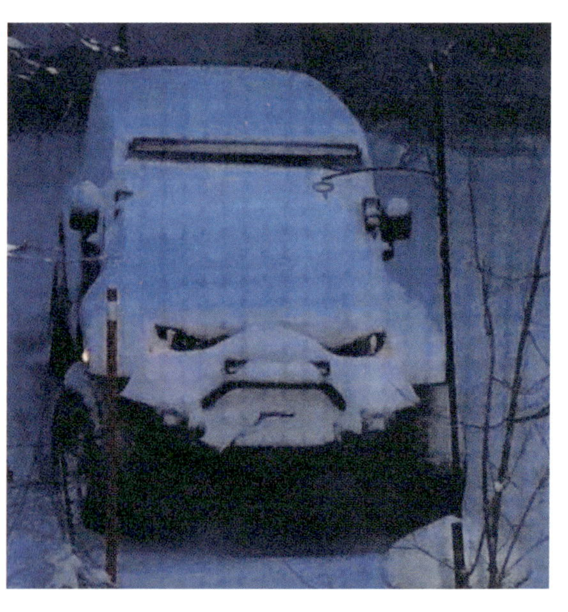

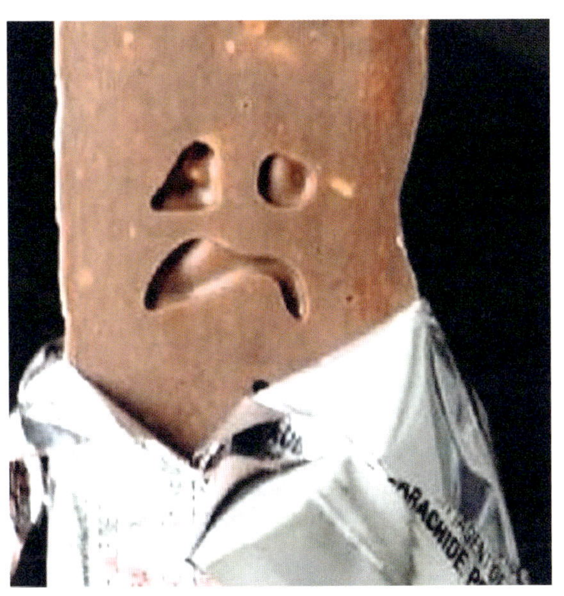

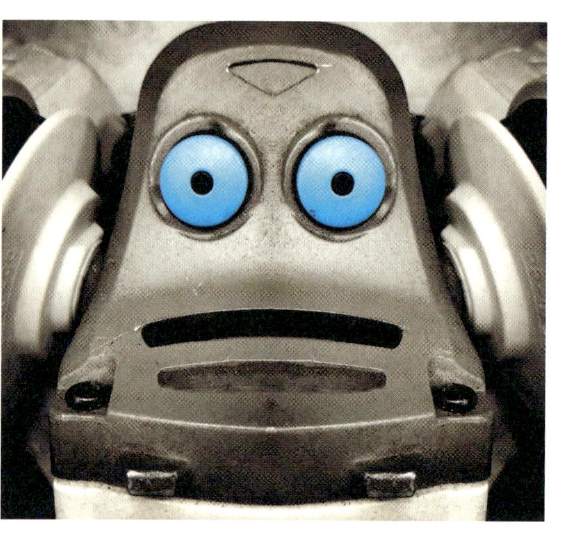

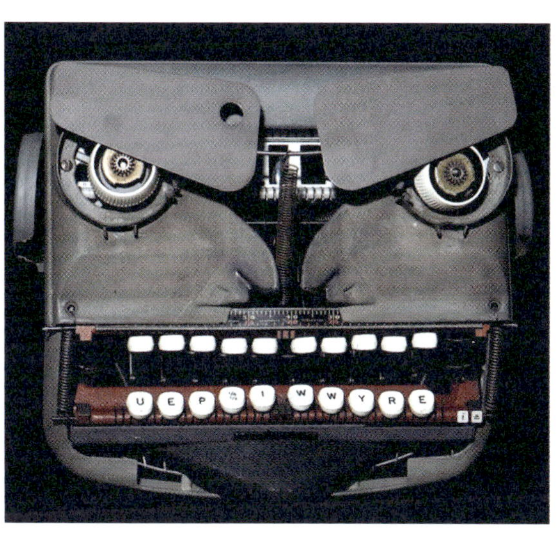

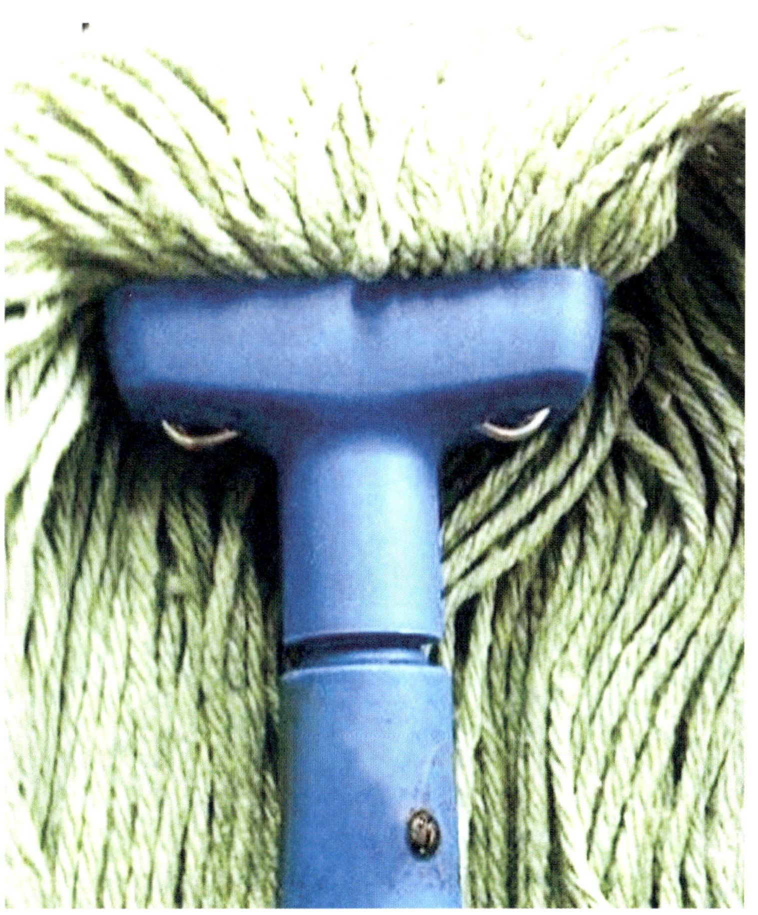

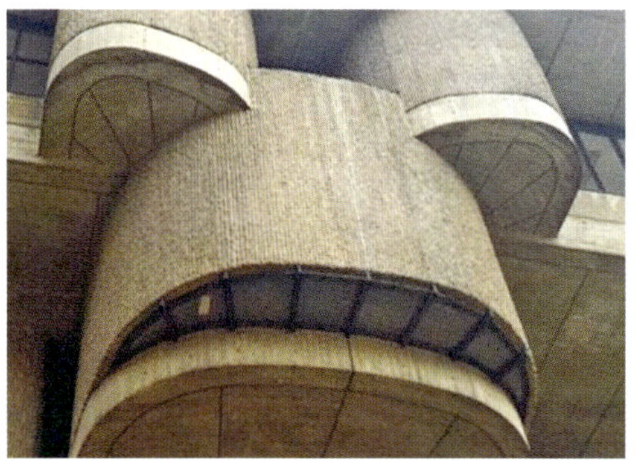

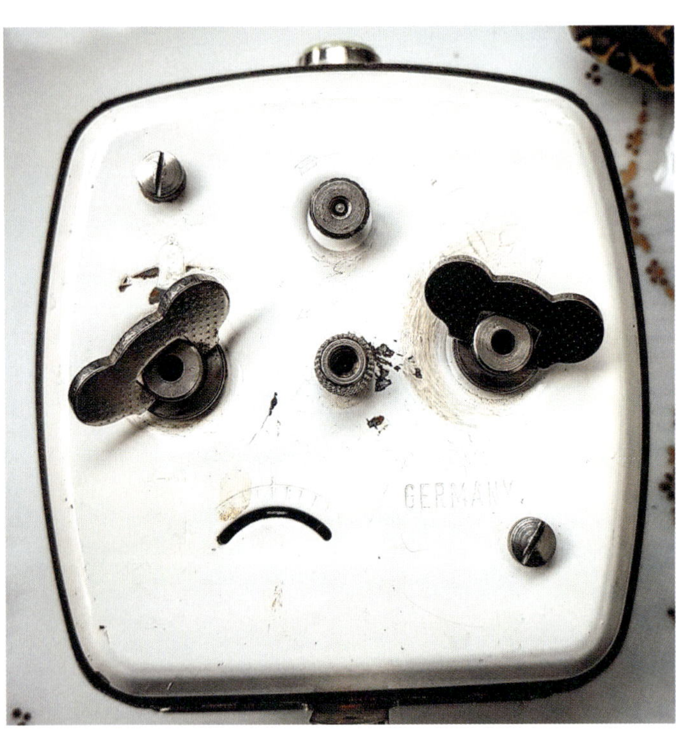
GERMANY

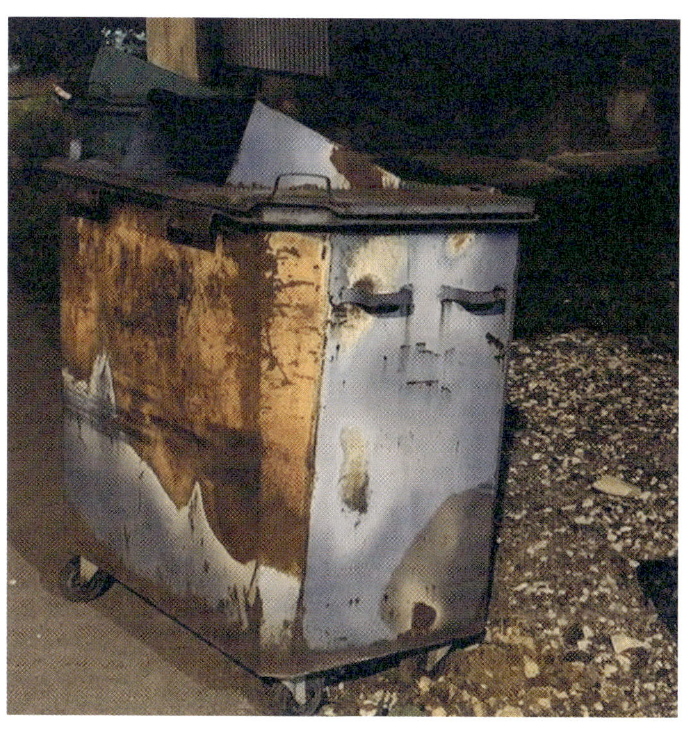

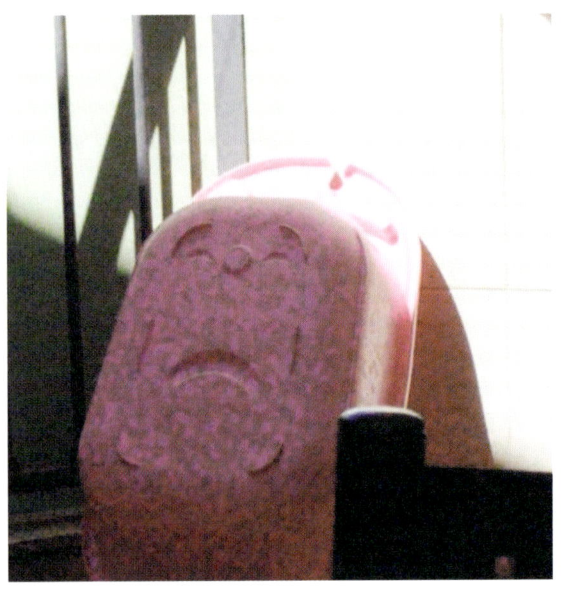

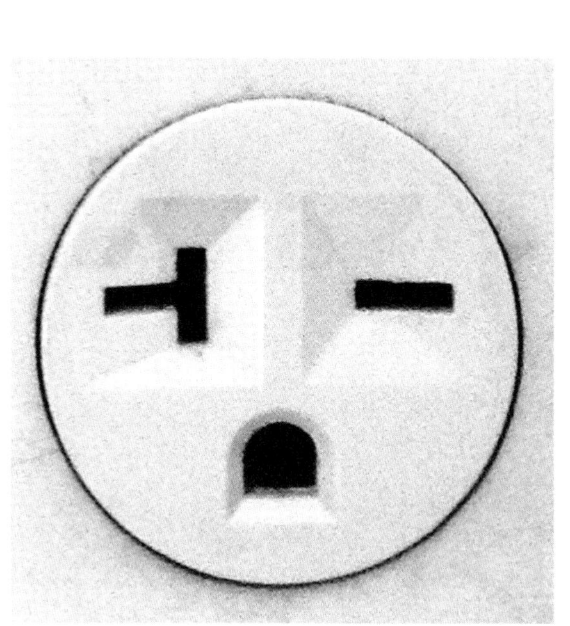

I SEE

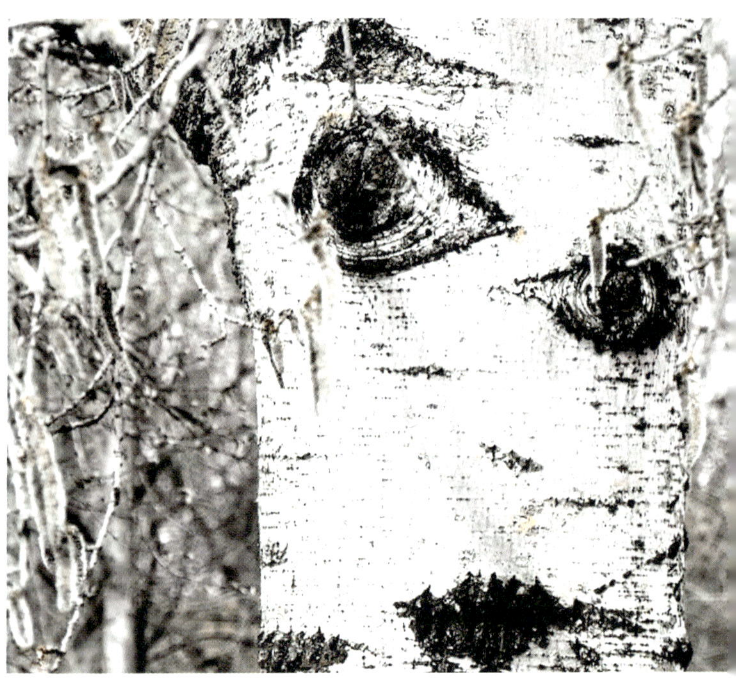

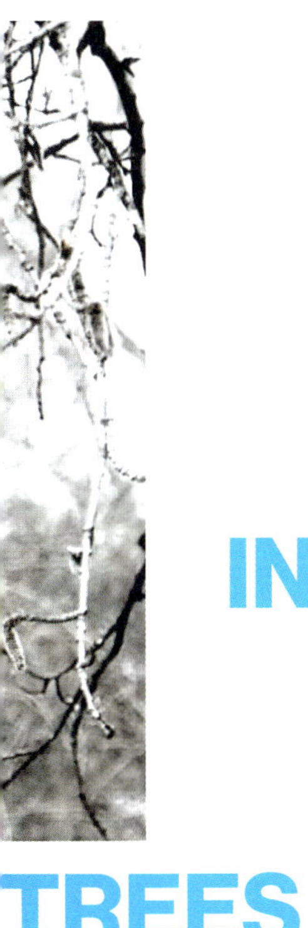

FACES IN TREES

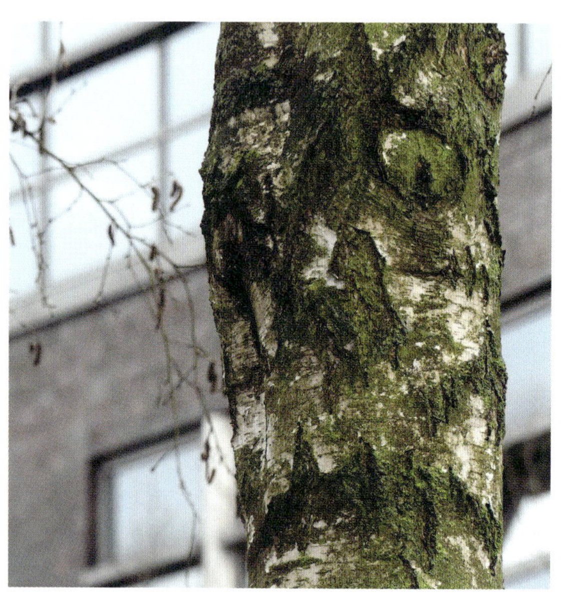

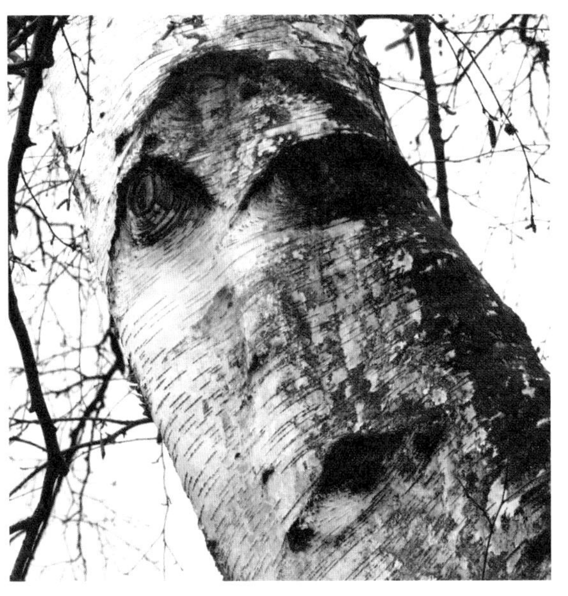

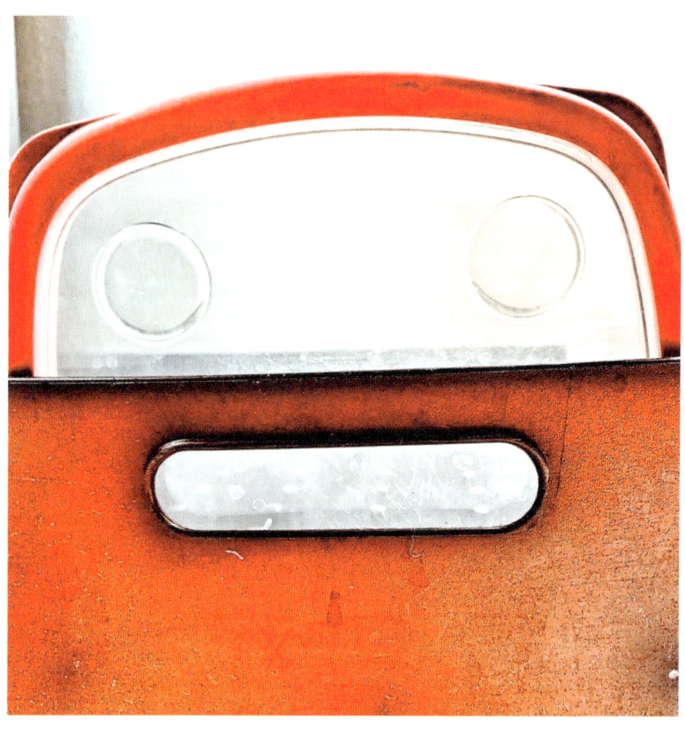

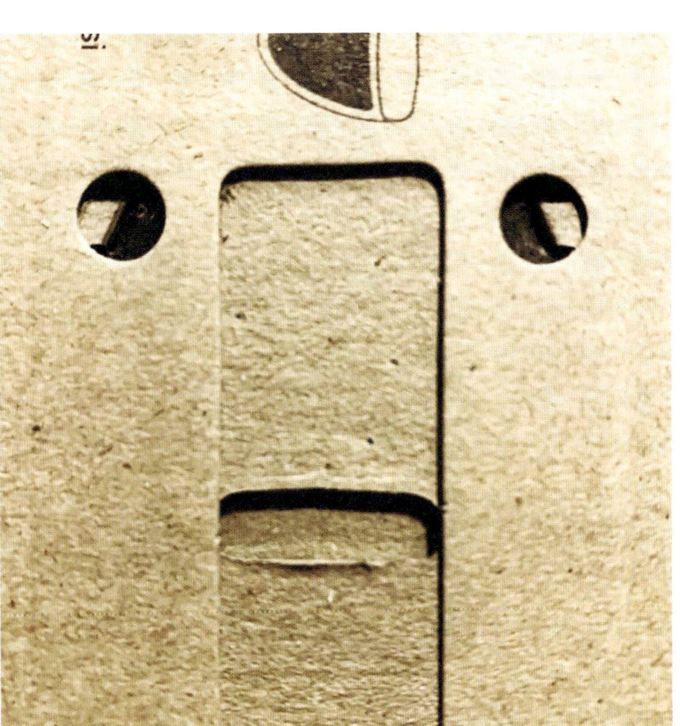

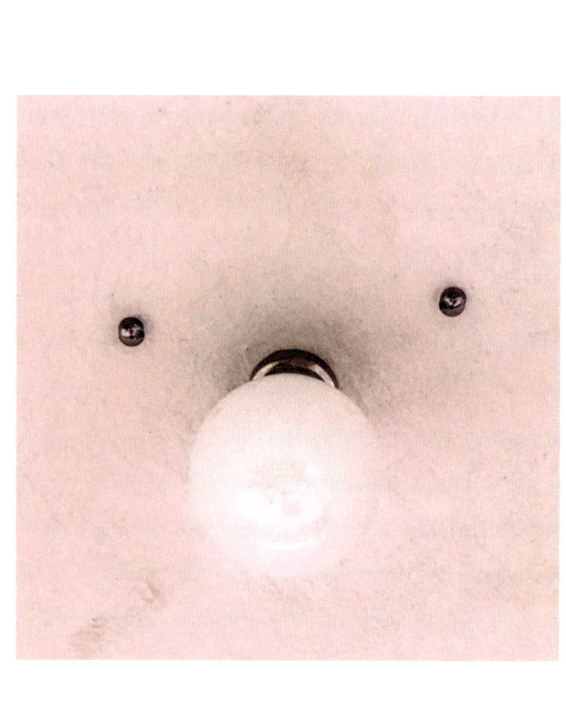

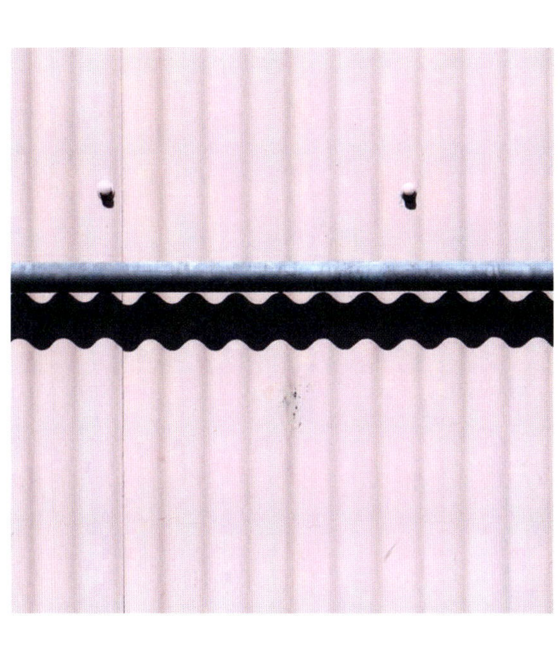

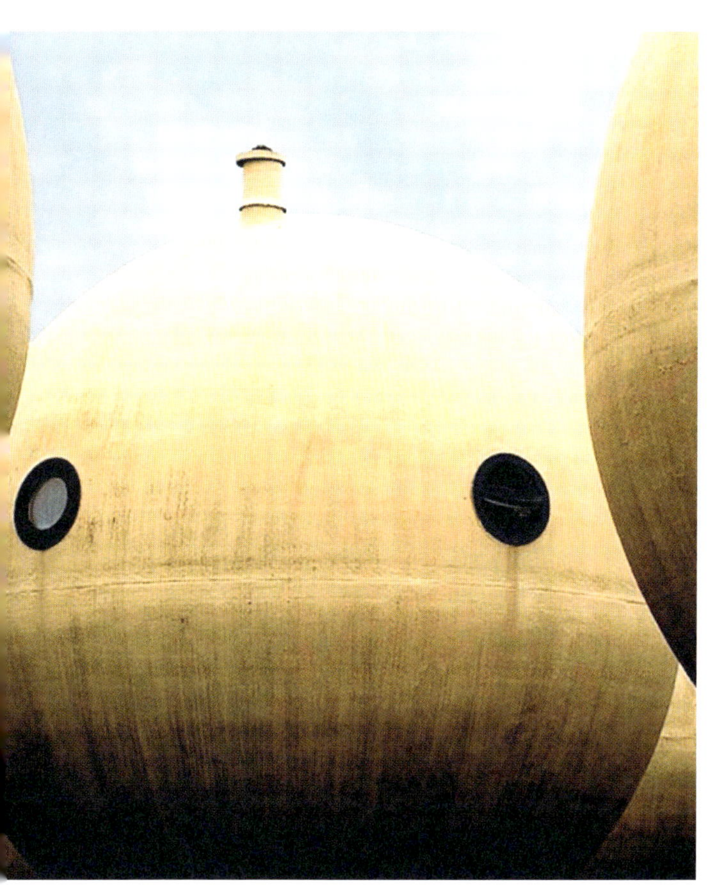

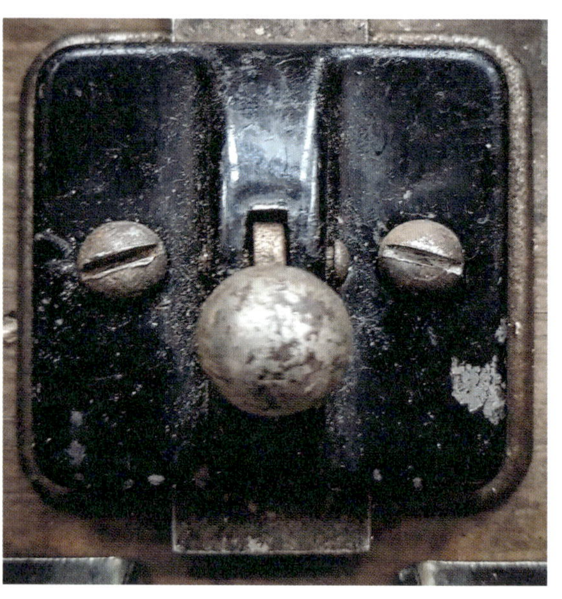

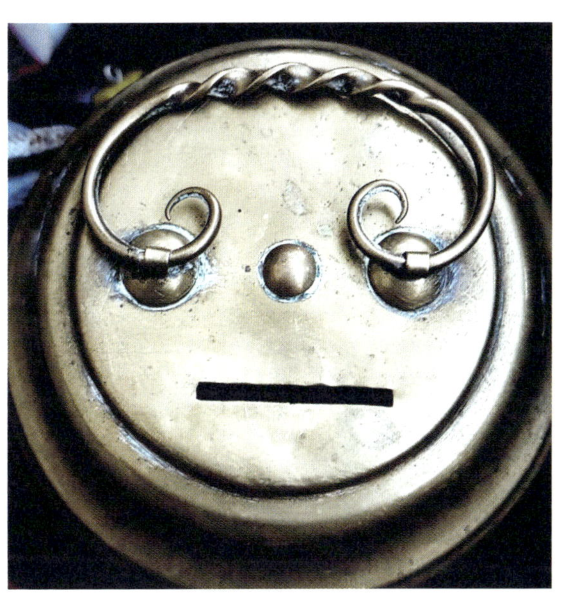

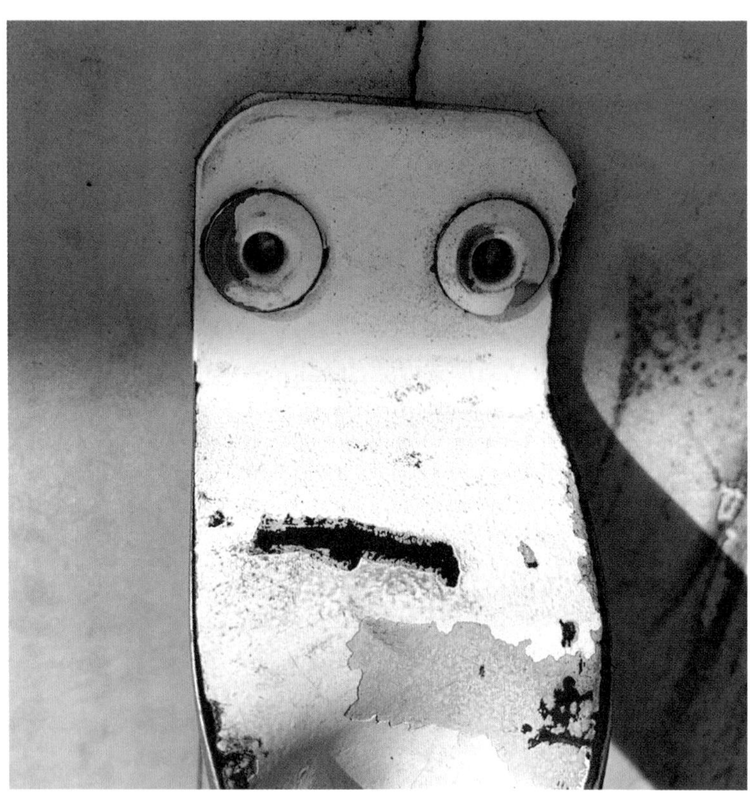

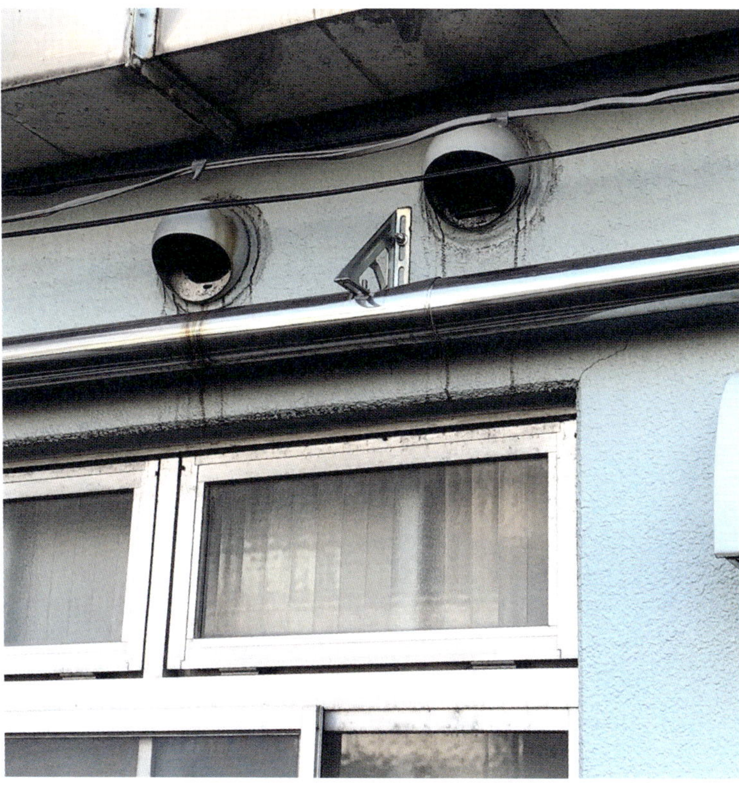

I SEE

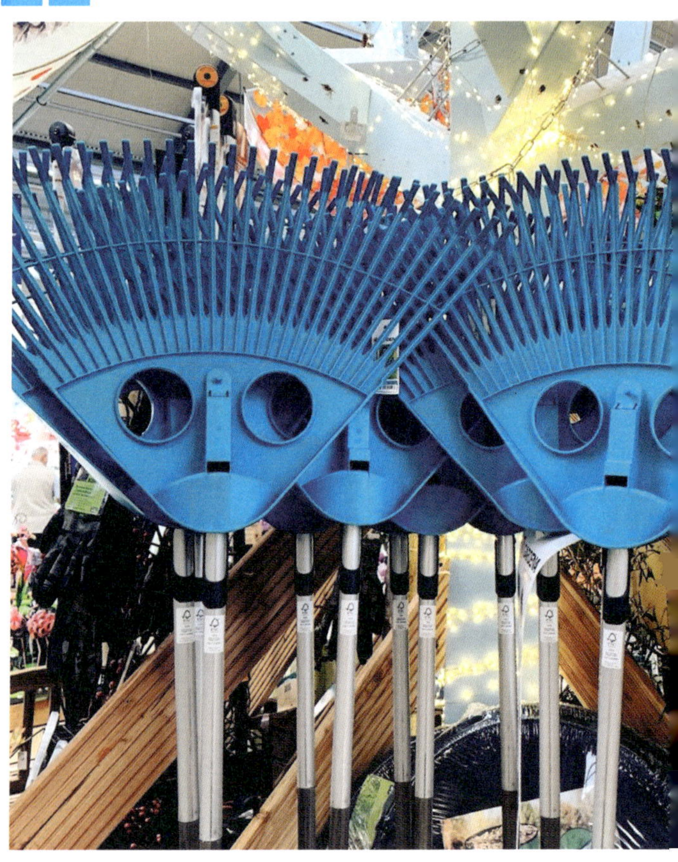

OF PLACES

FACES

IN THE

WEIRDEST

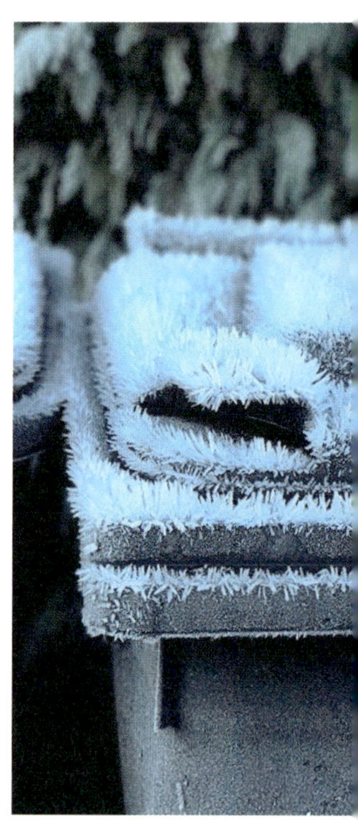

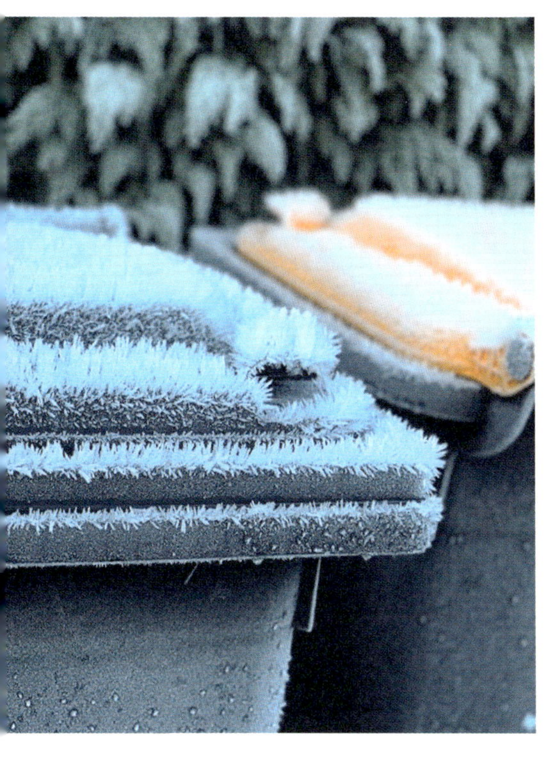

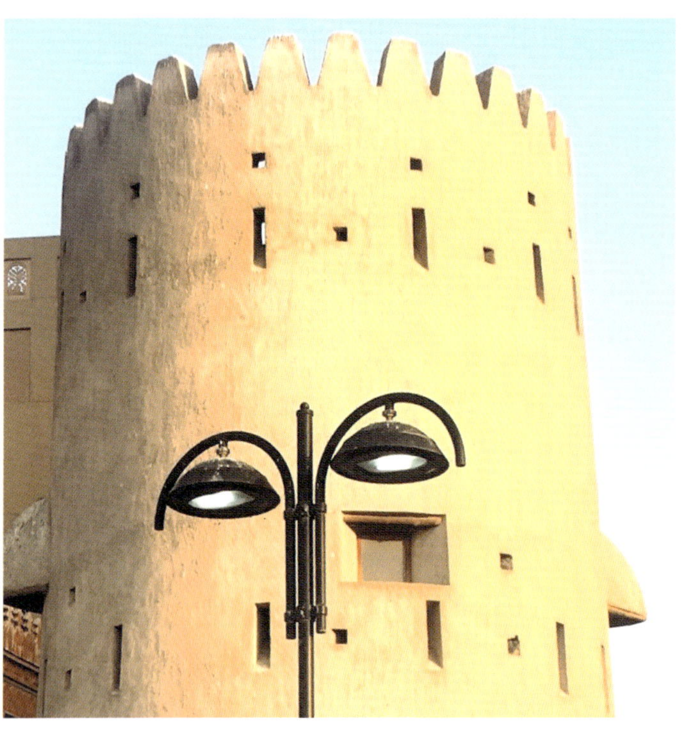

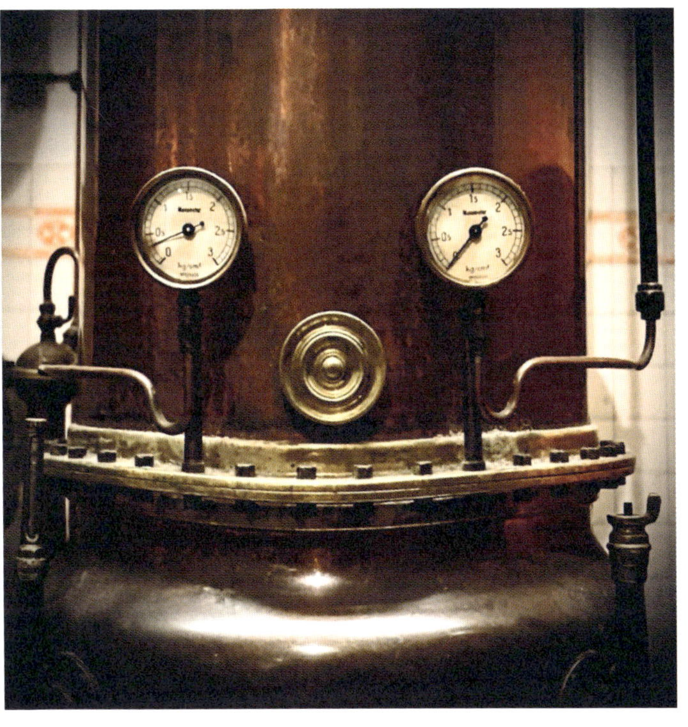

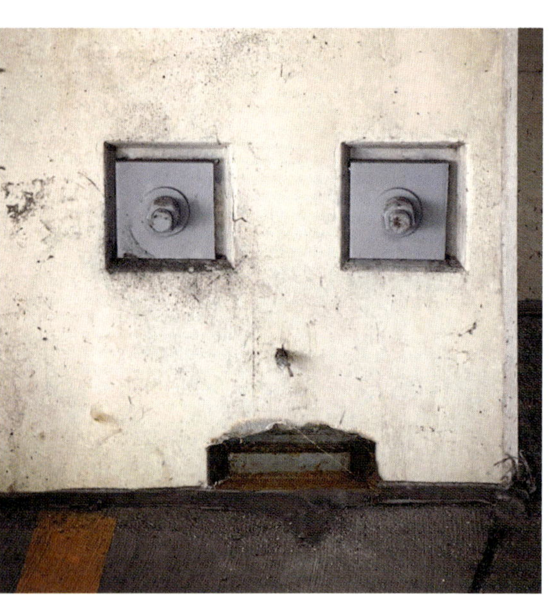

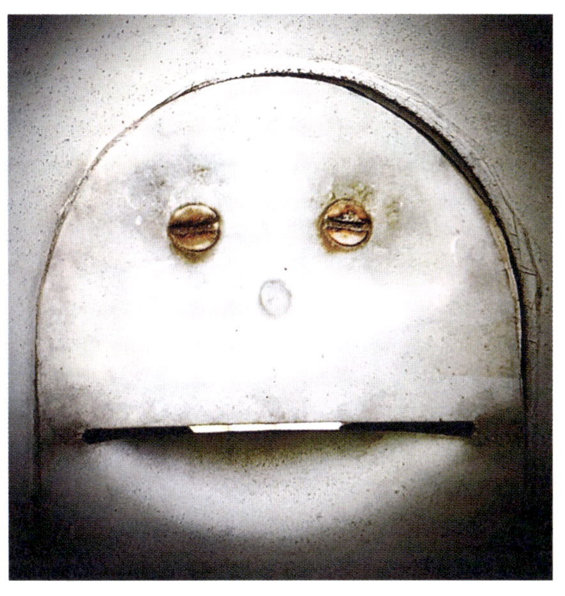

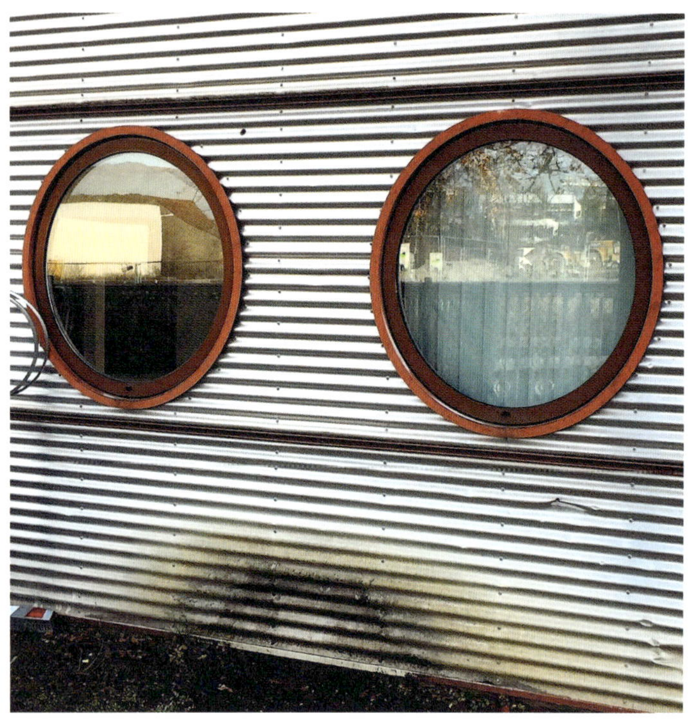

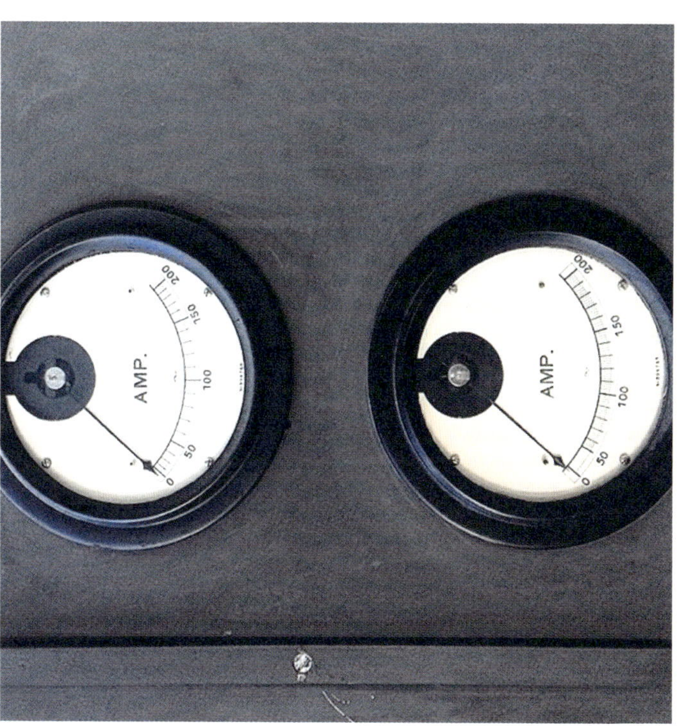
AMP.
0
50
100
150
200
AMP.
0
50
100
150
200

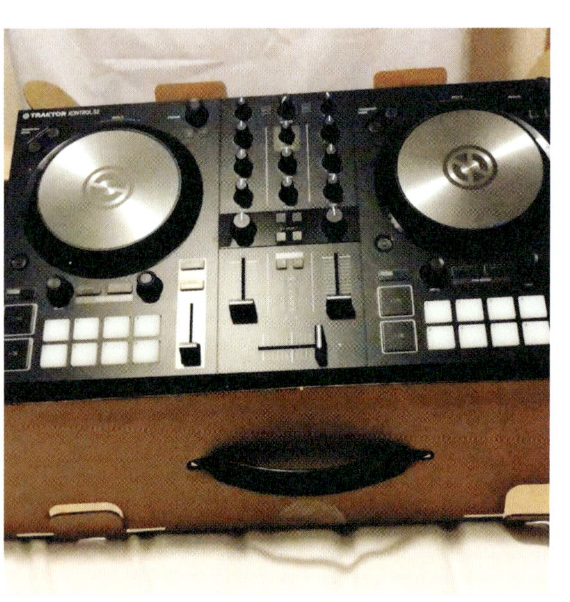
TRAKTOR

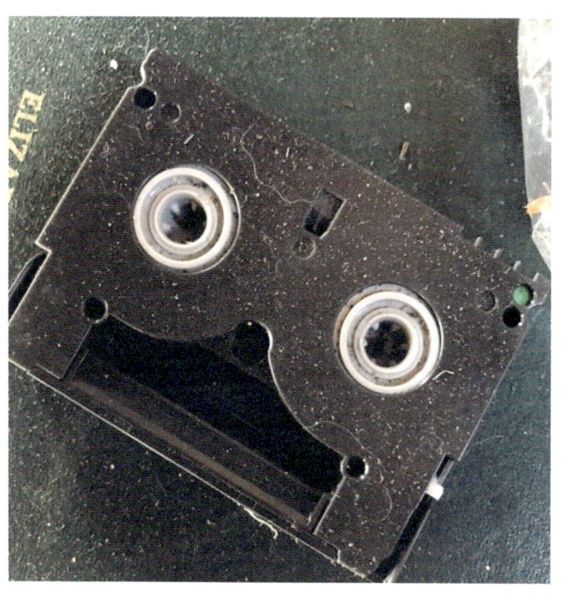

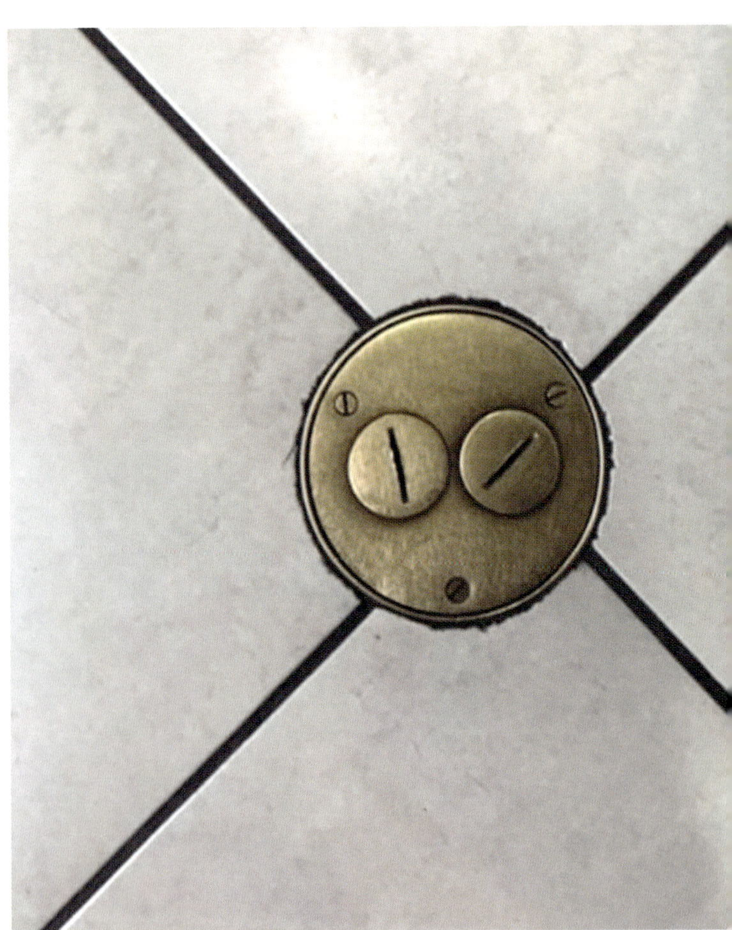

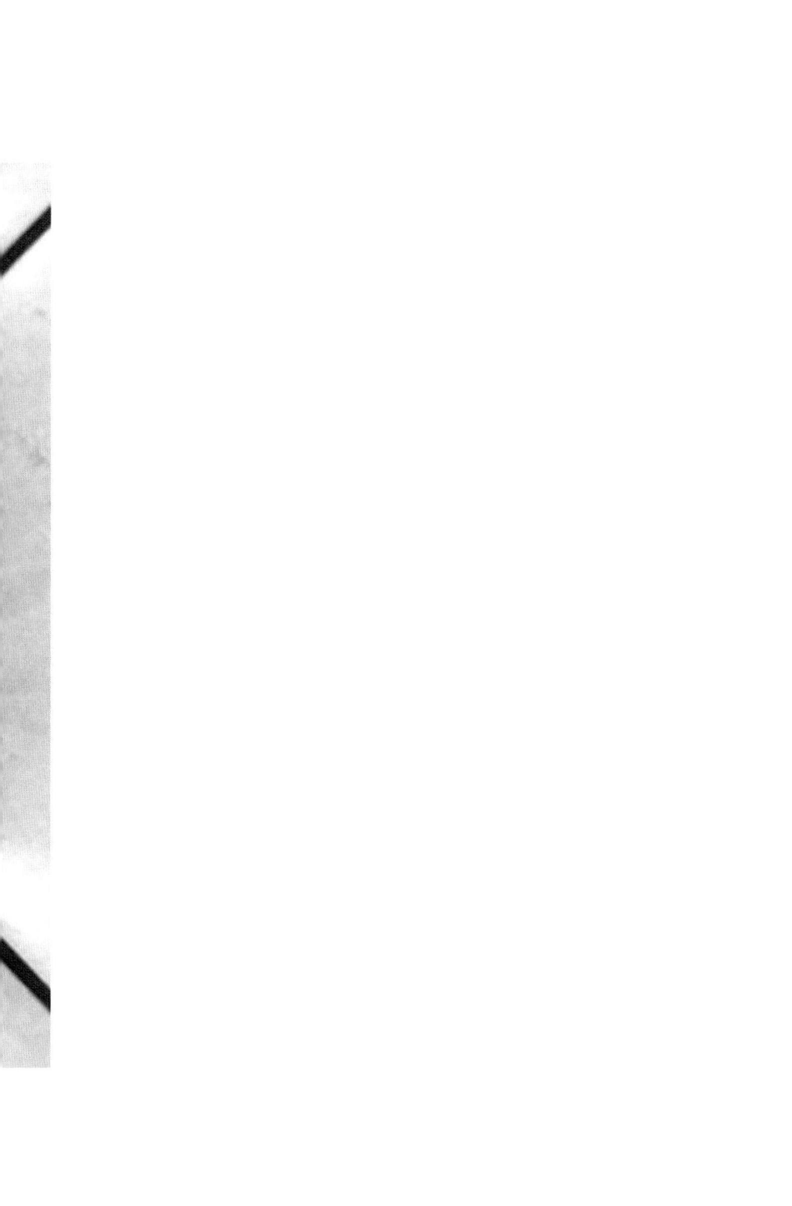

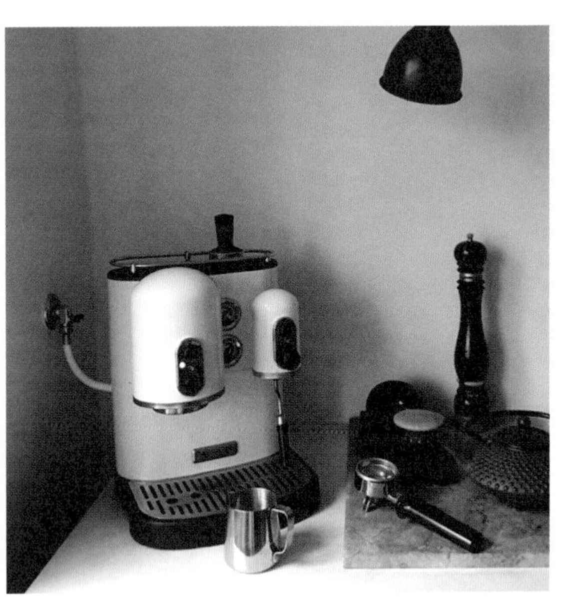

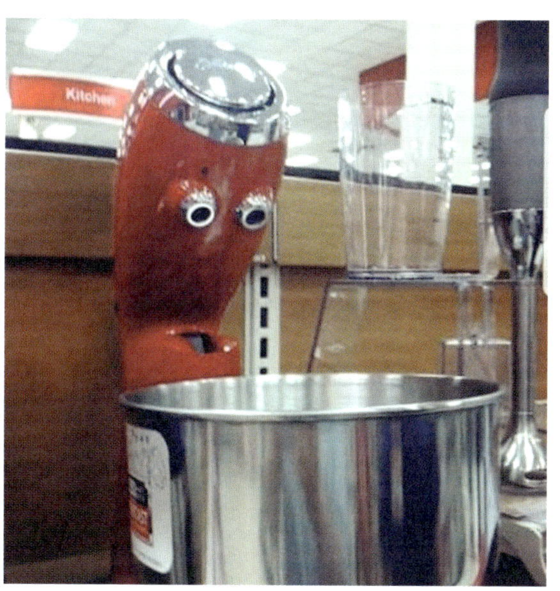
Kitchen

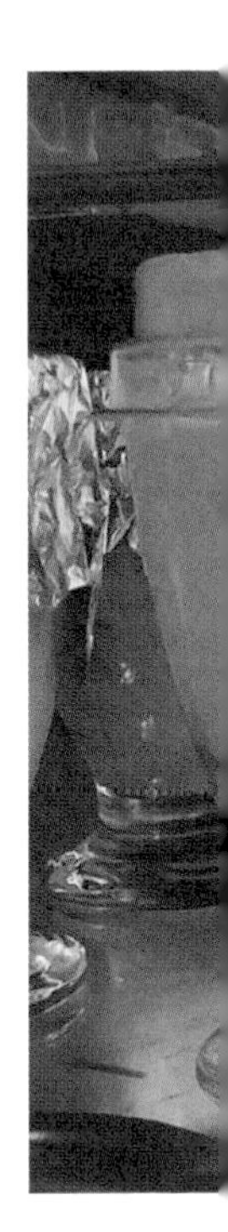

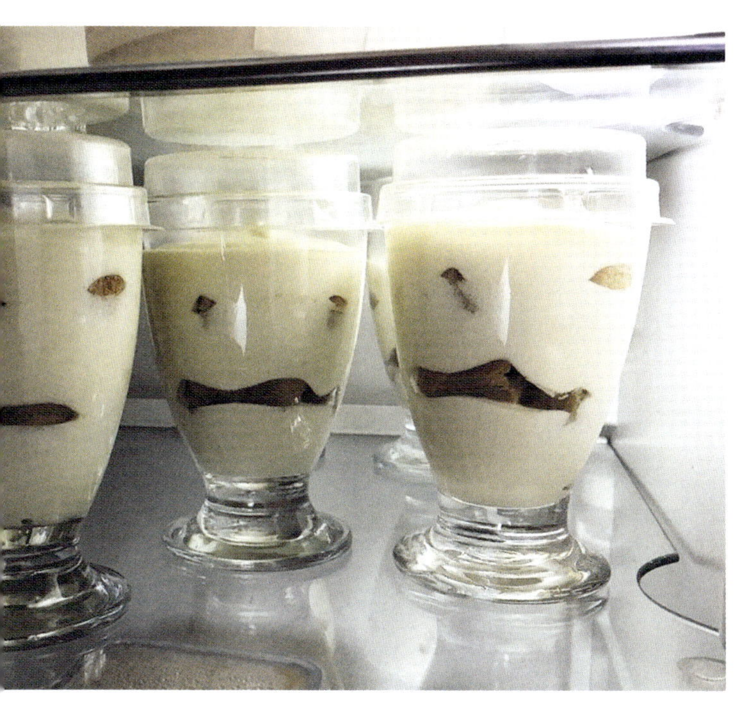

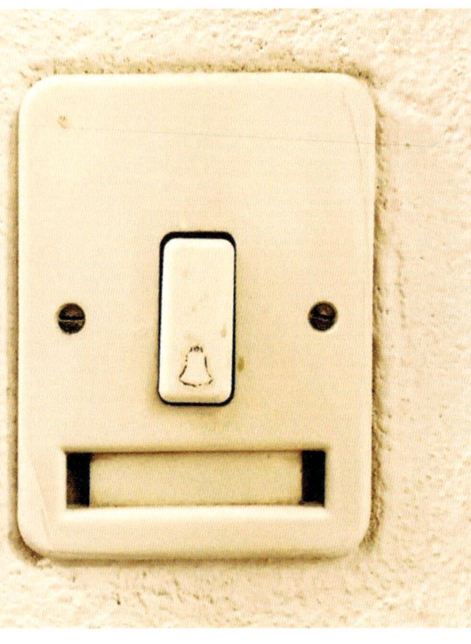

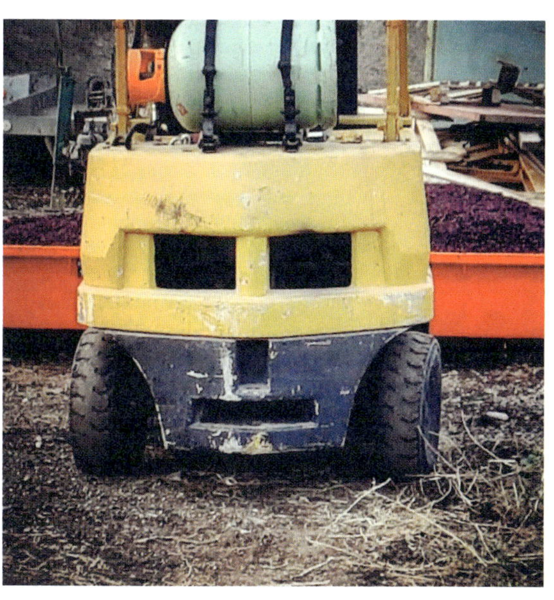

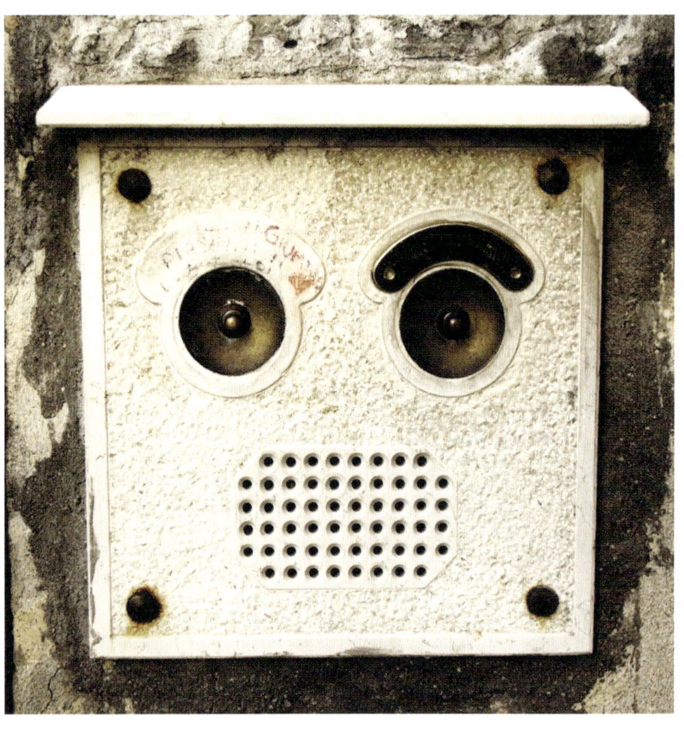

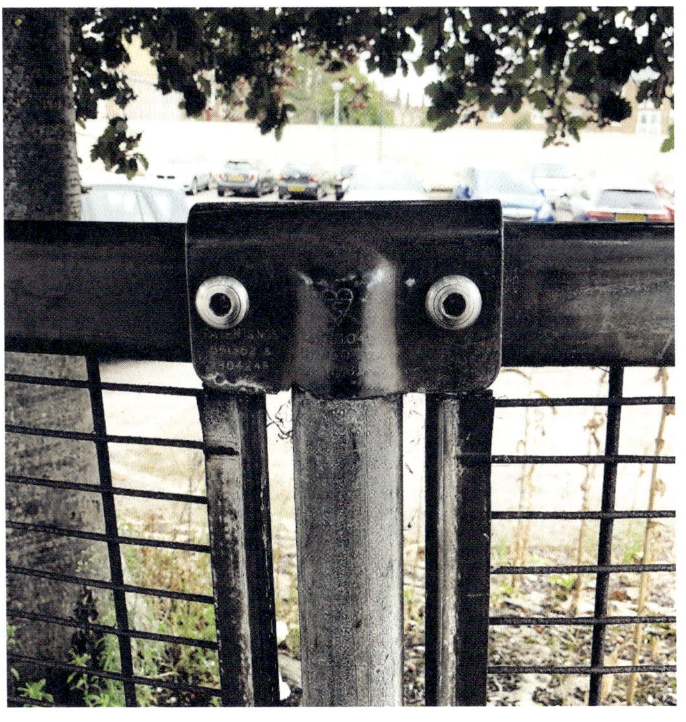

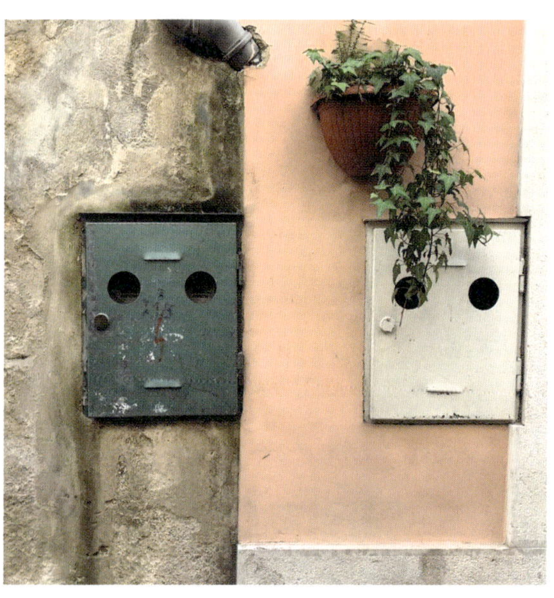

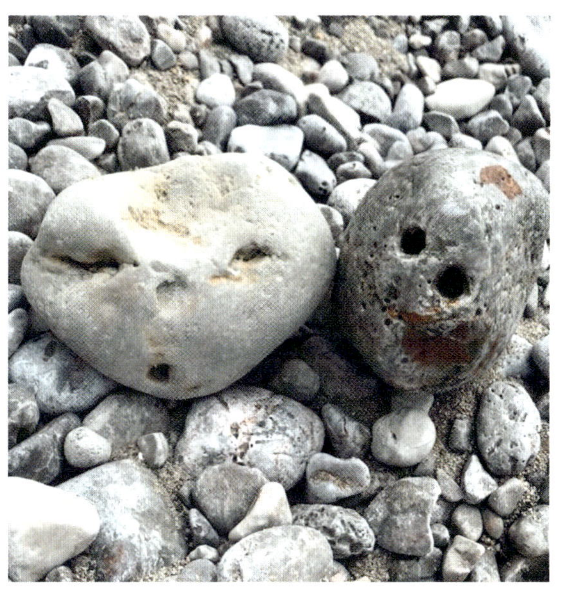

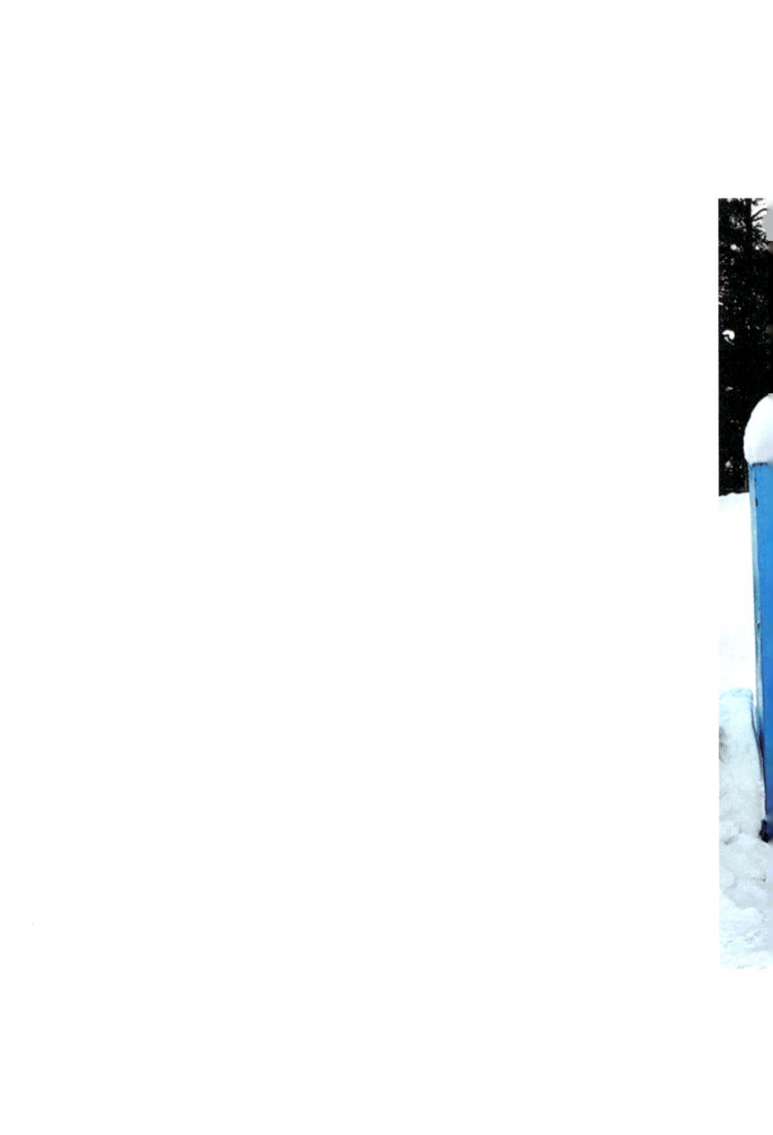

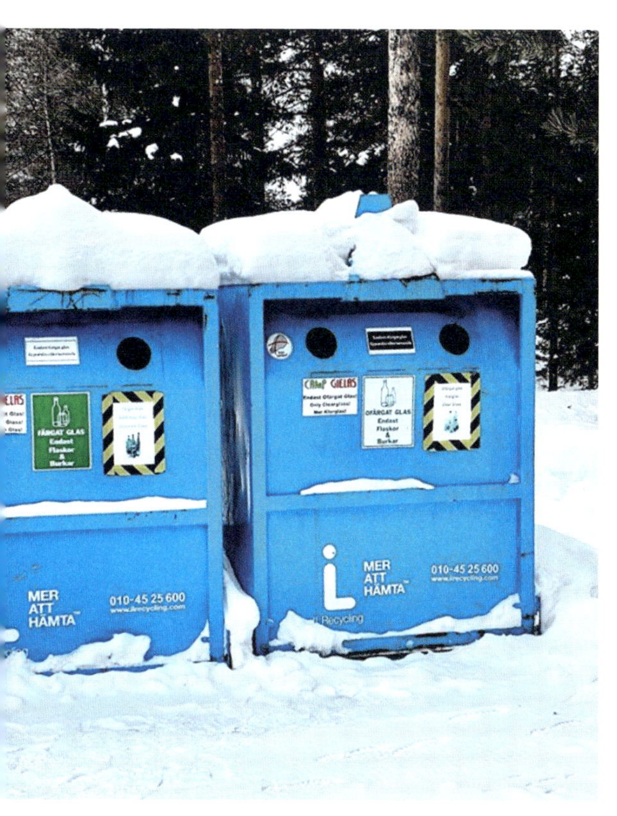
FÄRGAT GLAS
Endast
Flaskor
&
Burkar
MER
ATT
HÄMTA™
010-45 25 600
www.ilrecycling.com
CAMP GIELAS
OFÄRGAT GLAS
Endast
Flaskor
&
Burkar
MER
ATT
HÄMTA™
010-45 25 600
www.ilrecycling.com

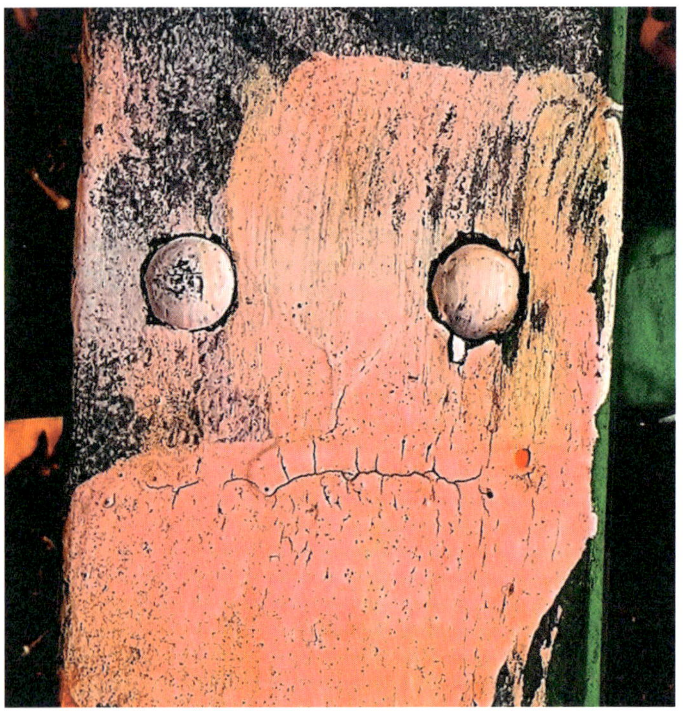

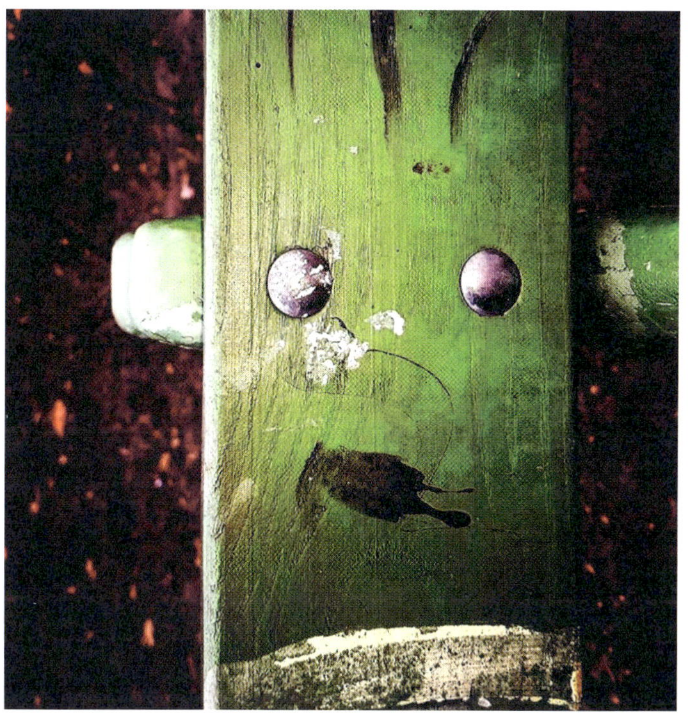

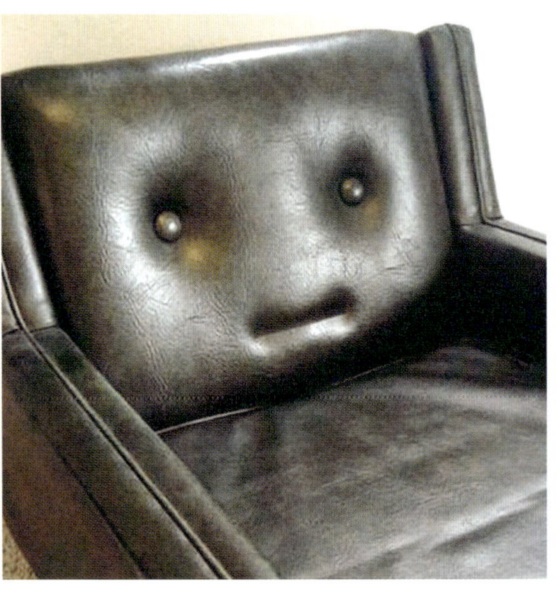

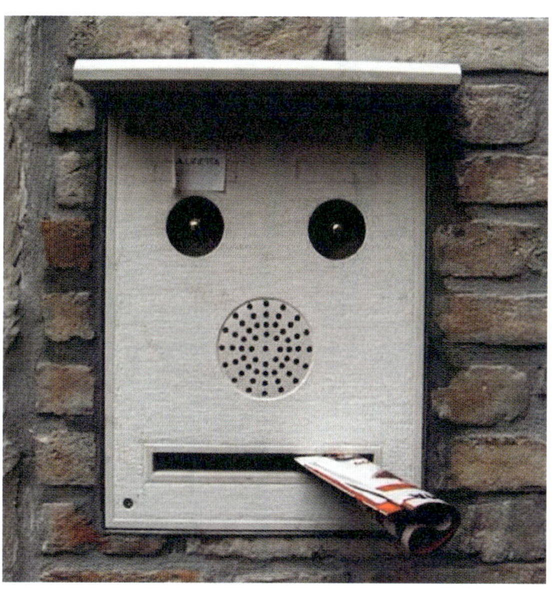

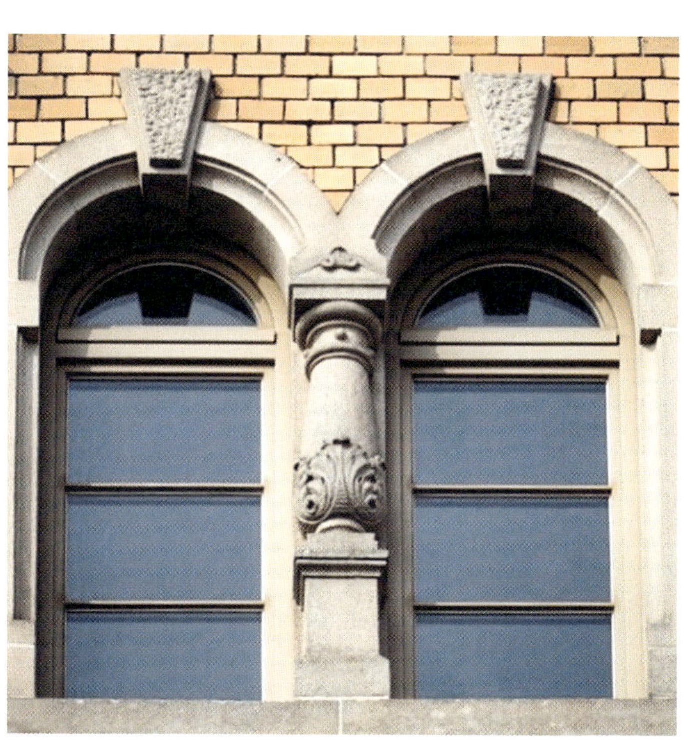

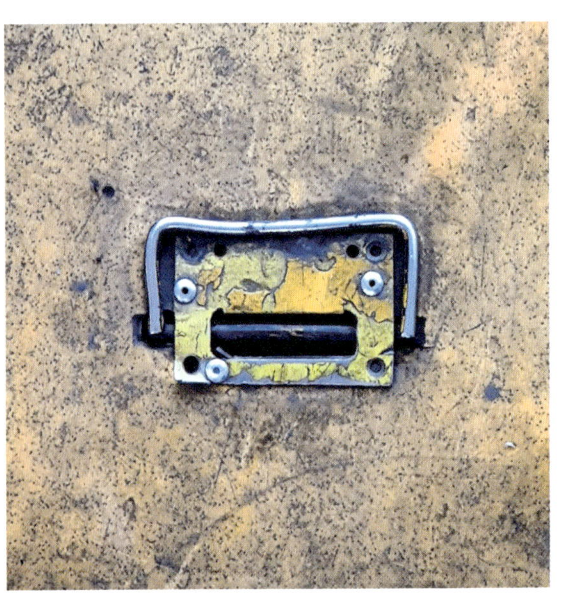

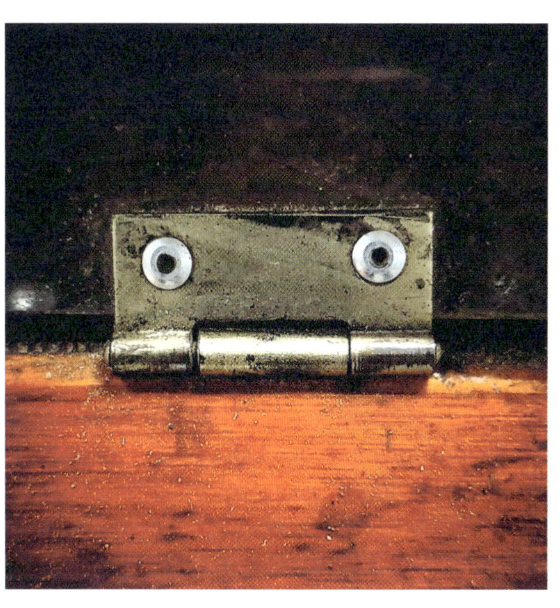

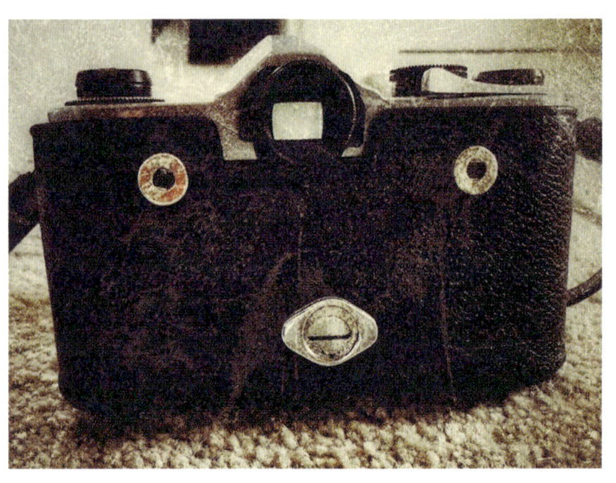

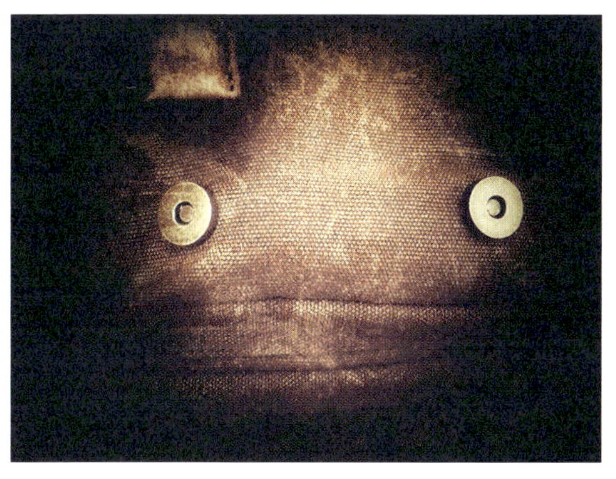

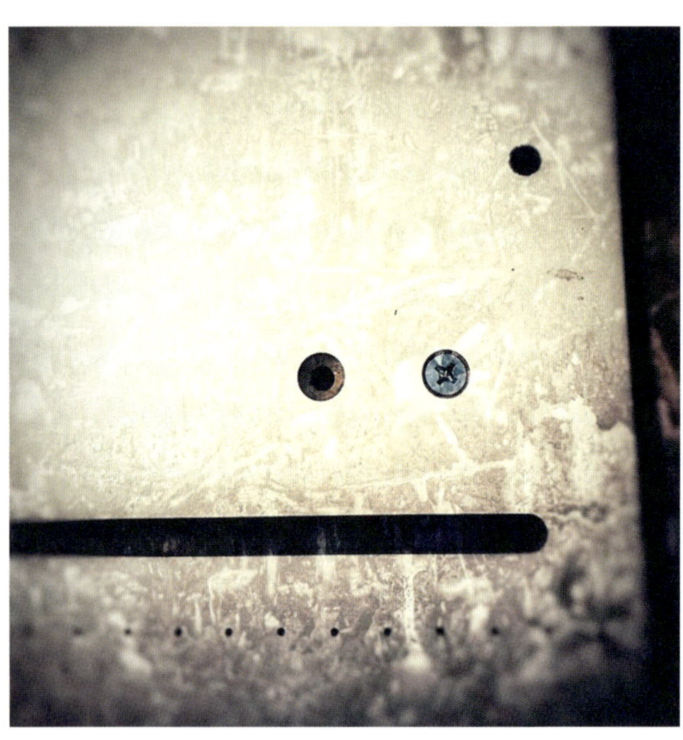

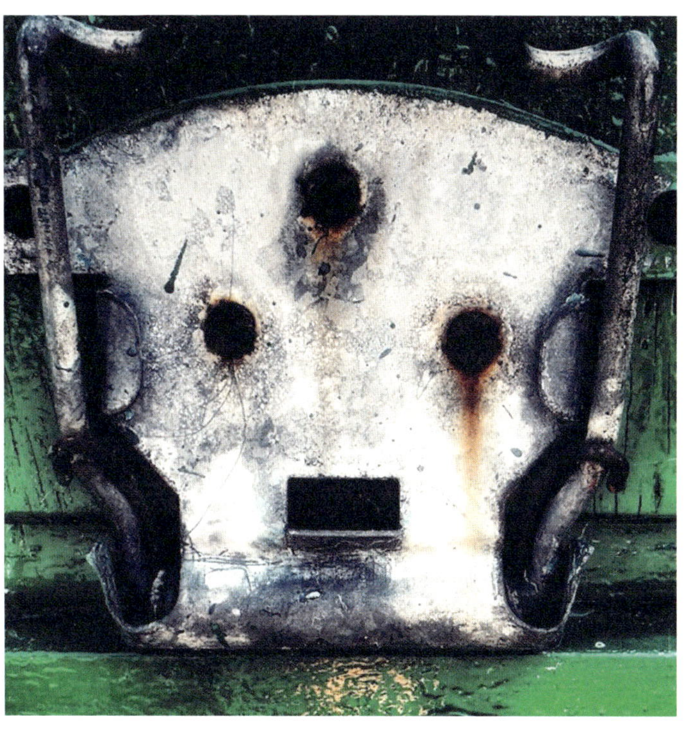

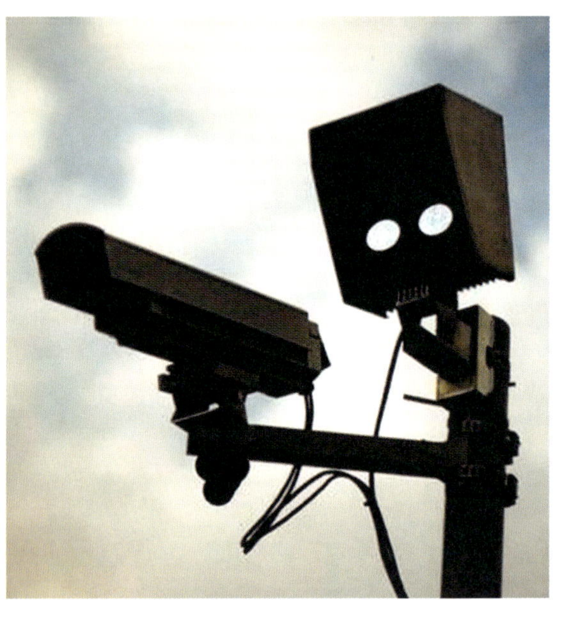

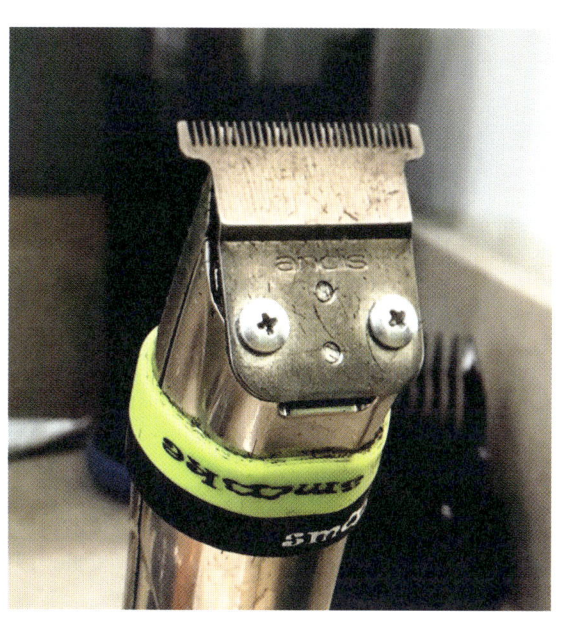

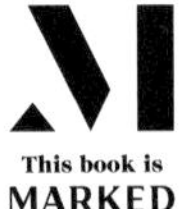

MARKED is an initiative by Lannoo Publishers
www.marked-books.com

Sign up for our MARKED newsletter with news about new and forthcoming publications on art, interior design, food & travel, photography and fashion as well as exclusive offers and events.

Photo Selection/Book Design: Irene Schampaert

Photo credits:
pp. 6 – 7 @mollo.berlin / p. 8 @martin12341806 / p. 9 @phersona /
p. 10 @tempestafoto_faces / p. 11 @maxlippolis / p. 12 @facesclaus / p. 13 @stonefish_dr /
p. 14 @xichty / p. 15 @mindfulfaces / p. 16 @pareidolia_art / p. 17 @tronderslarsson /
p. 18 Ruggero Blasi (@ruggero_buggero) / p. 19 @transcendtheobvious / pp. 20 - 21
@slignav / p. 22 @iseefaces_everywhereman / p. 23 @stonefish_dr / pp. 24 – 25
@polweg / p. 26 @cryptic_visuals / p. 27 @boris.sees.faces / p. 28 @facedbook /
p. 29 @facedbook / p. 31 @graugram / p. 32 @things.faces / p. 33 @inanimate_bob /
p. 35 @stonefish_dr / p. 36 @xichty / p. 38 @inanimate_bob / p. 39 @inanimate_bob /
pp. 40 - 41 @caritas_en_todo / p. 42 Marc Boudreau (@mackboude) / p. 44 @ros /
p. 45 @slignav / pp. 46 - 47 @engclau / p. 48 @elpadrino39 / pp. 50 - 51
@face_de_tronches / p. 54 @boris.sees.faces / p. 55 @boris.sees.faces /
p. 56 @sosopilami / p. 57 Tim Santhouse (@timsant) / p. 59 @nuriapuigs /
p. 60 @martin12341806 / p. 61 @martin12341806 / p. 62 @dreamerdoll_ /
p. 63 @nsimdrb / p. 64 @facedbook / p. 65 @facedbook / p. 68 @johnekroll /
p. 69 @jntcamille / p. 70 @karolinabadz / p. 71 @facedbook / p. 72 Airbus /
p. 73 @pareidoliapic / p. 74 @xichty / p. 75 @i.see.faces.every.where / p. 76 @stef_1140 /
p. 77 @xichty / p. 78 @somethingtodeclare / pp. 80 - 81 Sasha Wilson /
p. 82 @martin12341806 / p. 83 @martin12341806 / p. 84 @thelighthouselooksback /
p. 85 @thelighthouselooksback / pp. 86 – 87 @things.faces /
p. 88 @due_occhi_e_una_bocca / p. 89 @pareidoliapic / p. 90 @many._.faces /
p. 91 @many._.faces / p. 92 @anyelinaskartados / p. 94 @pareidoliapic /
p. 95 @caritas_en_todo / p. 97 @faces_object / p. 98 @luisa_di_buti /
p. 100 @lianatrifo / p. 101 @lianatrifo / p. 102 @thevjoiners_facesinplaces /
p. 104 @cara.tura / p. 105 @cara.tura / p. 106 @facedbook / p. 107 @facesofrotterdam /
pp. 108 - 109 @thevjoiners_facesinplaces / p. 110 @facesofrotterdam /

p. 111 @mildly_face / p. 112 @pareidoliapic / p. 113 @pareidoliapic / p. 116 @things.faces /
p. 117 @fslucas_photography / p. 118 @youlljusthavetofaceit / p. 119 @koolaz /
p. 120 @trashstarbybladee / p. 121 @leelu151 / p. 122 @pareidoliapic /
p. 123 @pareidoliapic / p. 124 @boris.sees.faces / p. 127 @_erfun_ / p. 130 @facesclaus /
p. 131 @things.faces / p. 132 @augustus_jonathan / p. 133 Christian Bork (@facogram) /
pp. 136 – 137 @drueckher.foto / p. 138 @drueckher.foto / p. 139 @drueckher.foto /
p. 140 @facearoundyou / p. 141 @facearoundyou / p. 142 @xichty / p. 143 @snfshoots /
p. 146 @facesclaus / p. 147 @facesclaus / p. 148 @knicholas_knockolas /
p. 149 @mstottfaces / pp. 150 – 151 @faceorama / pp. 152 – 153 @polweg /
p. 154 Andy Vital (@virtualvital) / p. 155 @facedbook / p. 156 @facedbook /
p. 157 @facedbook / p. 158 @inanimate_bob / p. 159 @inanimate_bob /
p. 160 @hiddenwonders01 / p. 161 @itsayslibby / p. 162 @alfv233 /
p. 164 @katrinemartensenlarsen / pp. 166 – 167 @nathaliedeweerdt /
p. 168 @faces_object / p. 169 @face_de_tronches / p. 170 @cara.tura /
p. 171 @cara.tura / p. 172 @facey6 / p. 173 @facey6 / pp. 174 - 175 @stefankleeberger /
p. 176 @photoartbykittyfischer / p. 177 @photoartbykittyfischer / p. 178 @facespics /
p. 179 @facespics / p. 181 @inanimate_bob / p. 182 @caritas_en_todo /
p. 183 @caritas_en_todo / p. 184 @martin12341806 / p. 185 @martin12341806 /
p. 186 @martin12341806 / p. 187 @martin12341806 / p. 189 @tempestafoto_faces

If you have any questions or comments about the material in this book,
please do not hesitate to contact our editorial team: markedteam@lannoo.com

D/2020/45/367 - NUR 653
ISBN: 9789401467247
www.lannoo.com

#AREYOUMARKED

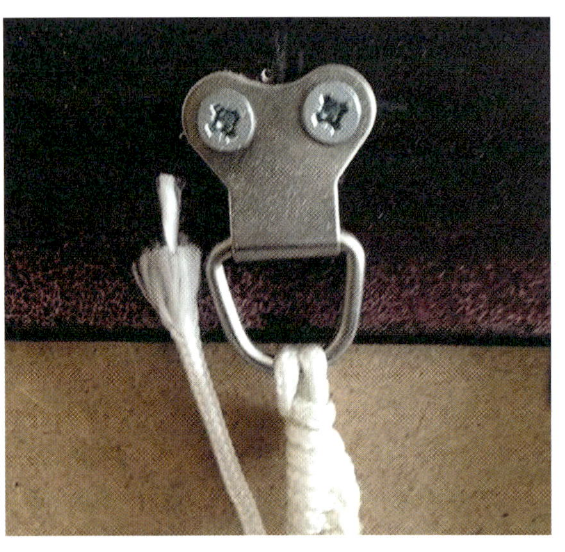